How To Solve A Crossword

Colin Parsons

CORONET BOOKS
Hodder and Stoughton

First published in Great
Britain in 1988 as a Coronet
paperback original

British Library C.I.P.

Parsons, Colin
  How to solve a crossword.
  1. Crossword puzzles.
  Solution – Manuals
  I. Title
  793.73'2

ISBN 0-340-43079-6

Printed and bound in Great
Britain for Hodder and Stoughton
Paperbacks, a division of Hodder
and Stoughton Ltd., Mill Road,
Dunton Green, Sevenoaks, Kent
TN13 2YA. (Editorial Office: 47
Bedford Square, London, WC1B
3DP) by Cox & Wyman Ltd.,
Reading, Berks.

ACKNOWLEDGEMENTS

I should like to thank Peregrine Worsthorne of the *Sunday Telegraph*, and John Hepburn of the *Scotsman*, for their kind permission to quote from my puzzles that have appeared in those papers.

My thanks, also, to Sean Kirwan and Philip Badnall, of Wallington library, for help and advice.

Last, but by no means least, my most grateful thanks to the thousands of readers who, over the years, have written to me in praise, criticism and query.

CONTENTS

FOREWORD   ix

INTRODUCTION   1

A GUIDE TO THE CROSSWORD PUZZLE   3

IRRESISTIBLE IMAGES: Composite clues   5

SOUND COMMON SENSE: Homophones   33

HARRY OR BOB ABOUT? Anagrams   35

A LITTLE OF WHAT YOU FANCY: Cryptics   45

NOTES ON USING THE LISTS   53

LISTS   55

ANAGRAM INDICATORS   129

ONE- and TWO-LETTER GROUPS   137

INDEX TO LISTS   144

FOREWORD
by
Betty Kirkpatrick

Editor: Chambers Twentieth Century Dictionary

Just about everything in this day and age is subject to rapid change. Food, dress, morals, hobbies – all are part of the frenzied modern kaleidoscope. How refreshing that at least one of our national obsessions remains constant, our obsession with words.

This obsession takes different forms. Some of us view words as being in the same category as rare tigers or giant pandas, a potentially endangered species that must be protected at all costs from abuse, misuse or even so-called progress. Buzz words such as hopefully, ongoing, situation, state-of-the-art, have the preservationists positively leaping up and down.

True lovers of words, however, regard them as something to be cherished, something to be treasured as the mainstay of their lives. These are the people who eschew jogging, aerobics, exercise bicycles, disco-dancing and pumping iron to devote their lives to some form of word game.

Each Christmas seems to provide us with yet another new board game as the toy manufacturers strive with each other to reach new pinnacles of sales. All of these do all right for a time – but in a short while we all fall back on trusted family favourites.

Top of the favourite word game league is bound to be the crossword, if game is not too frivolous a term for something so diverse in its appeal. For a start, it is capable of being totally self-contained – puzzle, pen and solver are all that is necessary for combat to begin.

Of course refinements can be added to this basic kit. For example some solvers are more sociable than others and welcome group solving. Admittedly this can sometimes add to the fun of crosswords, if only because it allows us the self-indulgence of basking in our superior knowledge.

On the other hand it can sometimes detract significantly from the feeling of well-being that comes from successfully tackling clues alone. Whatever is the point of completing *The Times* crossword in fifteen minutes if it was someone else who did the lion's share of the solving? It is difficult to delude oneself, if not others.

Word lovers are often also book lovers and it is one of the joys of crosswords that they give us a bona fide excuse for acquiring a large library of reference books. Of course no excuse should be needed but as a nation we are still guilt-ridden about spending money on books.

The Everest climbers of the crossword puzzle scene may scorn the help of books. For them sheer talent, stamina and native wit, not to mention a bit of practice, are all that is necessary to pit one's strength against the unknown. Using reference books would seem to them like cheating in exams.

Others again, those who clamber joyously among the foothills of crosswords, welcome the added dimension that reference books bring to their hobby. How marvellous to get totally lost in a dictionary whilst seeking the answer to a clue! It may add to the solving time, but it is time profitably and gloriously spent.

One of the great charms of crosswords is the diversity of information on which they draw. Magpie minds which absorb just about everything they ever encounter are particularly suited to the art of crossword-solving. Names of obscure birds, archaic literary terms, trendy words for up-to-the-minute items of clothing, little-known presidents of eminently forgettable countries are all grist to the crossword fan's mill.

The wide range of dictionaries and encyclopaedias, the indispensable *Roget's Thesaurus*, the *Penguin Rhyming*

Dictionary, are all valuable aids in the struggle against the crossword. It is truly remarkable how much knowdge gleaned at such times will stick in your brain over the years.

But crosswords, particularly those of a cryptic nature, can seem an uncharted jungle to those unversed in negotiating them. Books, like compasses and machetes, are all very well but there is nothing quite like a navigator to guide you through jungles.

The author of the present volume is indeed a skilled crossword navigator and within its pages conveys not only a multitude of facts about crosswords but a good deal of the cunning necessary to get to grips with them. Expertise in any area is usually sorely bought and it is a real privilege to have it given to us so painlessly and wittily.

Anagrams in particular can cause great problems to the novice crossword-solver. For a start there is the major problem of how to spot what clues are actually anagrams. Many fruitless hours can be spent trying to make sense of clues which are in fact just a re-arrangement of the letters of a word or words.

One of the many valuable aspects of this book is the section on anagram indicators. What little tricks does the compiler insert to indicate the presence of an anagram? This information alone is worth its weight in gold and will add significantly to the reader's crossword expertise.

There is something immensely satisfying about successful crossword-solving. How sad that there are some people who never experience this satisfaction simply because they regard crosswords as being very difficult and beyond their comprehension. Indeed some even feel that they are simply for intellectuals.

The Magic World of Crosswords will alter these misconceptions. Crosswords can be a source of delight to everyone. All that is needed is a little guidance on the mystique associated with them and Colin Parsons provides this in plenty.

INTRODUCTION

Winston Churchill said, of Hitler, 'The enemy is crafty and cunning, and full of novel treacheries and stratagems... There is no dirty trick that he will not play.'

For Hitler, read 'crossword composers', and you have been warned.

We will use every trick imaginable but, unlike Hitler, we won't hit below the belt. Our armoury of deceit is vast, but we do have our own Geneva Convention. In this book, I will explain the rules, and the absence of rules, to equip you for the fight.

Crossword puzzle fans are aristocrats. With just a pen, they can become indifferent to the horrors of commuting, or the boredom of waiting. Like most successful English hobbies, it is a solitary pleasure and, in a world more and more given to group amusements, a retreat to individuality.

Crossword clues are the most condensed form of writing there is, and I won't let my comments diverge from that rule. Let battle commence.

A GUIDE TO THE
CROSSWORD PUZZLE

No matter what lists are supplied, they're quite useless until the nature and mystery of the cryptic clue is unravelled. In the next four chapters, all kinds of clue are examined and dissected to find out what makes them tick. There isn't an easy way to do this; after all, a clue is either cryptic, or it isn't and there is no middle ground. Therefore, to a certain extent, you have to go in at the deep-end first, but with each example there is a wealth of explanation, so you shouldn't have any trouble. It would be very easy for me to do what many practitioners of an out of the ordinary subject do, i.e. to try and cloak the whole thing in a cloud of impenetrable mystery. Solving crosswords is a bit like learning to drive; at the beginning it seems to need the brain of an Einstein but, after a little while, we find that it isn't really difficult at all, and that our initial effort has resulted in us having the world at our feet. So it will be with the crossword; so, without any further ado I'll leave you to the first example.

IRRESISTIBLE IMAGES:
Composite clues

Cut and run   (7)
Your first instinct is to answer this with ESCAPE,
DECAMP, QUIT or FLEE, but it says (7) and, anyway, this
is a cryptic crossword. Since you know it doesn't mean what it
seems to mean, what *other* possible way can you approach it?

It won't take you long to realise that the answer must be a
word that means both 'cut' and 'run'. Now that the words are
separate from the phrase, they become open to different
interpretations. From 'cut' meaning to leave, perhaps, to 'cut'
meaning to incise. And 'run' is no longer speed along, but
manage, maybe. Now you have to work through all the
synonyms you know for both words until you come across
one that answers both. This sounds like a big job, but it isn't.
As in a lot of crossword-solving, your subconscious will do
most of the work. I'll discuss that aspect of puzzles more fully
later on and, in the meantine, we'll search for the common
denominator.

'Cut' inevitably leads us to think of surgery, and
operations. And there you have it. To cut is to OPERATE,
which also means to run. From a clue that started out
describing running away, we come to cut surgically, and run
managerially.

Cryptic puzzle setters are always on the lookout for this
coupling of words that gives a misleading impression, and
this is another:
Spider and fly   (7)
The two go together so well, that is it difficult even to

approach the clue without breaking it down into its component parts. Let's reverse the order to get rid of the nursery rhyme aura: (Word for) fly and (word for) spider. Ask yourself what you know about a spider, and the answer must be that it has a web. It spins this web, and is, therefore, a SPINNER. As soon as you have that you will remember that a SPINNER is also an artificial fly used by anglers.

As early on as this, we can see that the cryptic clue must *not* be read *as a whole*. There are exceptions in the pure cryptics, but as a general rule you must think in terms of breaking a clue down into its two or three basic units. The clue will have been given an image that more or less compels your mind down a certain path, and it is getting you out of the habits of a lifetime that I want to concentrate on in the next few pages.

Bill and Nick   *(5)*

In this one two men are suggested, but when you start to analyse the two words, it will be necessary to appreciate that Nick's capital N is a red herring, and that the word to concentrate on is plain 'nick'. Now, you can check your mental lists and see that to 'nick' is to cut or etch, and thus SCORE. This ties in very nicely with Bill in his invoice or reckoning sense.

These types of clue will not be confined to words linked by an 'and', but whatever the link word or phrase, the principle will remain the same, and should be borne strongly in mind when approaching the shorter type of clue.

Here we have a slightly different format, in what appears to be sound dietary advice to the portly:

Get thinner and lighter   *(5)*

It might seem that the clue is saying, (if you) get a word for thinner, you will also have a word for lighter, but this isn't so. We are still dealing with strict two-unit clues, so we are looking for a word that answers 'get thinner'. These aren't very thick on the ground, and we soon arrive at TAPER, which describes an old thin candle, or 'lighter'.

As with all cryptic clues, it is vital to recognise and attack them as separate units, with *nothing in common whatsoever*. It's a bit like cat and dog. We lump them together, but actually they are totally dissimilar. However, it is not until we can disregard the overall impression we have been given that we can approach them in a properly analytical manner.

In the clue above, the use of a comparative adjective for 'thinner' led you to imagine that 'lighter' was a comparative as well, whereas it was noun. The same trick is used here:
A lighter push   (5)
Once again, 'lighter' seems to be an adjective, but really it's a noun. In this instance, it is a river-vessel, which equates with BARGE, which also means to 'push'.

With this example, we have what seems to be a three-unit clue of some difficulty:
Ace, with Rod and Dick   (4–3)
Three chaps this time, two of whom are fakes. The punctuation and capital letters have been messed about with, and it should read: 'ace with rod (and) Dick'. Now that we see 'ace' and 'rod' without their human disguise, and without that misplaced comma, we find that we must solve the idea enshrined in the phrase 'ace with rod'. This seems to suggest a sharpshooter, a crack shot with a 'rod' or pistol. The way the number at the end is put, DEAD-EYE fits the bill nicely for *DEAD-EYE* DICK.

　　To sum up our early, but terribly important, venture into cryptic clues. A cryptic clue is a code. This code is hidden by what appear to be ordinary English phrases. This seemingly ordinary English is, in fact, a combination of units, *not* a coherent whole.

To pursue the mathematical idiom, we can think of the clue as an equation. The 'ands' and similar words taking the place of the equals sign. Thus we break down the clue into bracketed units, and arrange them in a quasi-algebraic form, as in this one:

$$(Register) \overset{to}{=} (do\ a\ job\ on\ the\ farm)\quad (4)$$

Here it is 'to' that plays the linking role, and the anwer is TILL. The (cash) register TILL, and to TILL the land. The overall idea the clue gives, however, is that one signs on ready for farm work.

You will find very quickly, that you do this compart-mentalising without conscious thought, but I would like to go through some more examples to fix the principle and the process.

Went like sheep to be searched   *(7)*
In other words, the phrase for 'went like sheep' equals ('to be') the same as a word for 'searched'. The answer is FRISKED. Note the suggestion of the passive voice in 'to be searched', although the solution is in the active voice, to FRISK.

Likewise:
R. Mugabe gives offence   *(7)*
isn't a racist slur on the boss of Zimbabwe, but merely coded instructions to tell you that 'rmugabe' has the necessary letters for ('gives') UMBRAGE, meaning 'offence'.

So, words like 'and', 'to', 'into', 'from', 'gives', 'produce', 'by', 'out of' etc., are simply to be regarded as meaning that one half of the clue equals the other half. Of course, this is by no means true on every occasion the word is used, but it will make you look at clues that contain them with a more critical eye.

A similar way of expressing the same idea is shown in this one:
The ornament is in the hold   *(5)*
This superficially suggests that a piece of jewellery is aboard a ship, but you will probably have guessed that 'in the' (word for) 'hold' is 'the ornament'. And you are right, CLASP being the answer.

Another form of deceit is demonstrated here:
Drops for a bit, then hangs   *(8)*
Despite the gruesome imagery of an old-fashioned execution,

we are still with the traditional two-unit clue, but instead of 'and' we have 'then'. That is to say, when you get the first part, 'then' you will have the second. But the way that it is phrased encourages you to think of a series of events. One thing happens, resulting in another. Naturally, this is all part of the conspiracy of mis- and disinformation that is the setter's stock in trade, but it is something else to be on the lookout for. The two parts of the clue are resolved like this:

$$\text{drops for a bit} \overset{\text{then}}{=} \text{SUSPENDS} = \text{hangs}$$

In the perfect world that crossword puzzle-composers would like to live in, these link words, although useful, are an impediment to the ideal clue. In Ernest Brahmah's *The Wallet Of Kai Lung,* a Chinese family are left a pearl of wisdom by a remote ancestor, and it is the job of the eldest son of every generation to reduce its length by one word, while in no way diminishing the truth that it contains. We setters strive towards the same pure goal.

This introduces us to another branch of the two unit clue, where the code contains no link words of any kind, nor is there as much as a single letter that isn't vital to the meanings. These clues *appear* still to have these conjunctions etc., but in fact they don't.

Green on remand   (7)
This suggests an individual who has transgressed, or seems to hint at the bilious hue any of us might have in such a situation. However, it is 'green' in the novice sense, i.e. UNTRIED. As you see, that also exactly answers 'on remand'.

Likewise:
Go ahead star   (4,3,4)
Ambitious Mr Redford it is not, but a definition of '(to) go ahead' which is TAKE THE LEAD, which, strangely enough, describes what it means (to get the role of a) 'star'. Once again, the phrase 'go ahead' is meant to mislead by hinting at 'go getting'.

With:

Hangmen sailing ships *(7)*

you can't help but visualise pirate captains murdering their wretched passengers, but the reality is more mundane: 'hangmen' (after the famous public hangman Jack Ketch) gives KETCHES = 'sailing ships'.

Reading this book, you are going to feel yourself secure against the composer's maraudings. But if you do, you are deluding yourself. These types of clue are a bit like phobic fears; you know it's silly, but conditioning takes over. You have to make a constant effort to resist straightforwardness and, unless you force your mind to tear such clues to pieces as a matter of course, they'll get past you.

Gets out the Water Music *(7)*

is a good example. Such is the power of your previous experience, that you will find yourself accepting 'Water Music' as an indivisible unit and, once the idea has taken root, you'll find it almost impossible to break the pattern. Once more, we have the false capitals to cause confusion. Had it been written like this: 'Gets out the water music', the illusion would be less compelling. As it is, we split the clue in an improbable place: 'Gets out the water' = STRAINS = 'music'.

In this one, the trick lies in punctuation:

A dropper of names, like Crippen or Palmer *(7)*

and suggests that the two worthies were guilty of that odious social vice (compared to which, a few murders are neither here nor there). Nonetheless, they killed people and were executed for their pains. That is to say, they took the 8 o'clock drop, so rewrite the clue correctly: 'A dropper. Of names like Crippen and Palmer'. A somewhat sanguinary clue for HANGMAN. Most people don't associate humour with crosswords, but there's a lot of it about! Looking at these clues in a vacuum, you are bound to think of them as having to be done as mental exercises, and you may well say, 'OK, I can see the working, *after you've explained it*, but how am I

10

expected to solve such complex logic problems in my head?' A fair question, and the answer is, you aren't. You'll find that you get at least half the letters you need by filling in other words. If you say that that sounds like a paradox, I must tell you that in any crossword, there are bound to be three or four that are 'easy'. That is to say, you will be able to solve them because you get an intuitive flash on a certain percentage of clues. By the same token you will sit and stare at something, subsequently seen to be 'obvious', for hours. Once you have this start, everything will fall into place.

Always remember that you have one tremendously important factor working in your favour. At the moment, you think that you know nothing about crosswords, and that's true as far as the subtleties of cryptics are concerned. But you have built up a lifetime's store of knowledge through reading and watching TV, and your subconscious is bursting with information that it will give up as soon as you ask it the right questions. You don't have consciously to realise that most words with the second letter T, start with S, or that a word with it last three letters 'o-s', is more likely to finish with 'ious' than anything else. That is all there locked away, and your poor old subconscious thought you'd never ask!

I must stress the importance of not going along with the conspiracy of deceit the composer has woven in his clues. Beware the seemingly composite phrase, as in this one:
In the ancient world, holy water was sacred to him (7)
'Holy water' has a specific meaning, as did 'Water music', and that is the trap. In fact, the phrase has to be separated, as: 'In the ancient world, holy' = NEPTUNE = 'water sacred to him'.

Like the swamp where the grass grows greenest, the more straightforward a clue seems, the more you must suspect it. Like:
Criminal chasing woman (7)
must lead you towards that class of person that includes muggers and rapists, but the truth, naturally enough, lies elsewhere. 'Criminal-chasing woman' = NEMESIS.

The suspicious thing about that one was the lack of an 'a' before 'woman'. It would have made the clue read much more smoothly, so you should have gone onto Red Alert when you didn't see it. You'll get the 'solver's nose' quickly enough, and then I will only be able to fool you half of the time!

In the next two examples, we see one that has a similarly suspicious look to its phrasing, and one that's a bit sneaky 'Ancient and Modern'.

Makes film shows the correct way   (7)

Makes movies by the book, perhaps? Isn't it interesting, however, that the composer says 'film shows'. You might well *see* a film show, but it isn't the expression you'd use if you made one. You would say film, or picture. Perhaps 'film shows' is a 'Water Music' type of trick. If it is, and we split the clue between the words, something might happen; here goes: 'Makes film.' 'Shows the correct way.' It won't take you a fortnight to arrive at DIRECTS, will it?

I won't labour the point, but just to recap briefly: clues that have no link words can either be two words that mean the same, or one word and a phrase, or two phrases. These groupings will have an overall sense, but this will be spurious. Often, but not invariably, what seems like a common expression will be a false joining of two totally independent words, as in this classic example.

Quick breathing   (5)

Here, we are using the old fashioned meaning of 'quick' (and the dead), and 'breathing', which means the same, ALIVE.

After the Test Paper, we will explore the rich vein of wit and cunning allowed by the Captain of the Men of Doom, the magnificent three-unit clue.

a) *Keen to get the flat opposite* (5)

This clue contains a phrase and a single word definition of the answer. Which is which?

$$A$$

b) *Post office workers* (5)

$$B$$

A combination of two common expressions; how would you approach it?

c) *Rose let down by her boyfriend* (5,2)

d) *People who nick money* (7)

Pure two-unit clues, or are there link words?

e) *Jersey person working in the sunshine* (7)

f) *Peach shop* (6)

How do you split the first, and how does the second compare with 'Quick breathing'?

SOLUTIONS (printed upsidedown!)

a)
The single word is 'Keen', as a definition of SHARP (opposite of 'flat' in music). The other contender was 'opposite', but a moment's reflection will have shown that 'to get' was the = phrase. It could not have been a pure two unit clue, because 'keen to get the flat' does not mean anything.

b)
'office workers'. a synonym for 'Post Office'. So it is 'Post' = STAFF = 'office workers'. There was no way of deducing whether A or B was the phrase, except for the fact that it would be hard to imagine

c)
'By' might have been the link word, but again, there is no real one word definition for 'rose let down' or 'her boyfriend.' 'Rose' is STOOD UP, which answers the balance of the clue entirely.

13

are not a significant grouping.

There are other kinds, and we'll look at them later, but they

1st	Three-unit groups
2nd	Anagrams (a variety of three-unit clue)
3rd	Pure cryptics
4th	Two-unit clues

Two-unit clues account for the smallest percentage of cryptic clues. The largest single group you'll meet are the three-unit groups, with anagrams and pure cryptics providing most of the rest:

* * *

This clue, which is obviously two single word definitions, is like 'Quick breathing', because it uses an archaic word that means the same as its modern equivalent. The answer is INFORM, and both 'shop' and 'peach' are verbs which mean (to) INFORM (on). It is interesting to notice how some words which have long ago died out of common usage, still survive healthily in their combinations, so to speak. Gotten is thought of wholly as an Americanism, yet we use it all the time in phrases like 'misbegotten' and 'ill-gotten gains'. Peach, which died out with Dickens, can still be found in impeach. Gorm (more properly gaum) is meaningless until it appears in 'gormless'; and so on.   (f)

The impression of a Channel Islander enjoying the fine weather is, it goes without saying, a misleading one. A person working in the sunshine might perspire and be a SWEATER = 'Jersey'. There was no need for a false capital, as Jersey had been made the first word, and it is worth noting that composers will alter the structure of a clue to achieve this, so look out for quaintness or contrivance in a clue that starts with a proper name.   (e)

Surprisingly, the overall answer is in contrast to the spirit of law and order, because 'those who nick' is a vernacular way of describing COPPERS, also a type of money.   (d)

In three-unit clues, the full power of the composer's imagination (or cunning) is set free, and they are probably the most interesting and complex of all the groups.

This type of clue contains two smaller clues, and a definition of the word that is the answer, as in

Knight served up fish and meat cake   *(7)*

On the Round Table, of course! There is only one knight who features sometimes in crosswords, as a part indicator, and he's KAY. However, he's a rare visitor, and doesn't seem relevant here. Since there is no particular knight to aim at, we must assume that it is the generic name for knight, SIR. Now it looks as if he 'served up fish'. That line has to be abandoned, because there isn't a word for 'served up fish'. The 'served up' is a hint, though, and it would seem likely that 'served up' means the same as 'put up' (to write backwards) and 'served' has been used because of the food connotation. So now we have RIS. Do we now think of a fish and meat cake that starts with RIS? Well, yes and no. We are looking for a cake of some kind, but probably just a meat cake, the fish being needed to get the second part of the word. Obviously, it is SOLE. The RISSOLE is a meat cake, and we were put off by its apparent linkage with fish.

Do keep in the forefront of your mind at all times, that the nuts and bolts of the clue will, where it is humanly possible to do it, be disguised in phraseology in keeping with the theme. It will say 'served up', because its a food clue. In this example:

Hock; its about right for a cocktail   *(5)*

the use of the word 'cocktail' drives your mind into the rut of thinking of 'Hock' in its alcohol sense. In fact, 'hock' here means (to) PAWN, and it is 'about' (written around) 'right'. Crosswordese for right is R. Thus, when we write P r AWN, we get a type of cocktail.

So don't automatically look for obscure meanings just because the phrasing isn't general. If the composer wants to reverse a word in a clue that deals with the army, he will say 'retreated'; if its about horses, he will use 'backed', and so on. English has such a vast reservoir of synonyms, that it is possible to find one that is suitable for every occasion, but you must learn to recognise them for what they are.

In this example, we can see how a clue is artificially split up to seem like a statement.

Imagine! A ship bringing me a perfect lover (9)

Which has a nice Bobby Shaftoe ring to it. When we look at it more closely, the first thing to note is that 'bringing me' is just a more roundabout way of saying 'and', making it an = word. With that gone, we are left with three units. Let's strip them of what seem to be superfluous words, and get

A	B	C
Imagine	*ship*	*perfect lover*

Therefore, the clue must be: A + B = C or A = B + C.

On balance, since the answer cannot be the second word, B, it would seem that 'perfect lover' must be the definition, because there are so many synonyms for the idea. 'Imagine', on the other hand, doesn't seem to have anything in the nine-letter range. 'Imagine' is fancy, invent or dream. There may be something in fancy, but it doesn't look hopeful, invent is useless, but dream suggests 'perfect', and if we add BOAT/'ship' to it, we have the young lady's swain from the main.

This is a little more difficult, but we can still work on probabilities,

Surplus astrologers become supervisors (9)

Did they see it coming, one wonders? Again, it looks obvious that 'become' is the = word, leaving

A	B	C
Surplus	*astrologers*	*supervisors*

for your subconscious to work on. There are more words for 'supervisors' than there are for 'Surplus', so we must start with the idea that it is A + B = C.

'Surplus': excess, over, extra.

'Astrologers': fortune tellers, seers, gipsies.

Answer: OVERSEERS.

Here we have a more complex one, but something to get your teeth into, and to sound a warning note.

On army camp, time for lights out is 0336 hours (9)

The somewhat arbitrary time is suspicious, but let's see if we can get it by the book.

A	B	C
Army camp	*time for lights out*	*0336 hours*

Army camp: post, station, base, fort, depot, barracks.

There is no general time for lights out, so we want something more wide-ranging, which is obviously NIGHT. If we put that after FORT we have our answer, and a FORTNIGHT is twenty-four hours times fourteen days, or 336 hours.

As I said earlier, because the puzzle-setter needs FORT, 'army camp' has to be used; therefore he twists all other parts of the clue into a military posture. 'Dark' would have done for NIGHT, but 'lights out' harmonises so much better, and the whole thing is finished off by making a total of the hours in a fortnight appear to be a time of night used in the army.

Likewise, with this one, all the parts have been so phrased as to create an overall impression, totally at variance with the true meaning.

Given rifle, hurried and got the bullet (9)

Superficially, a clue suggesting the straightforward acquiring of ammo for a gun. However, the thing about this one that should make you suspicious is the phrase 'got the bullet', which is a peculiar way of putting it. There is no special type of bullet needed, so why not *a* bullet?

The answer is, that 'got the bullet' has a totally different meaning, and is nothing to do with weapons. In its other sense, then, that bit of the clue means SACKED, and before it we have 'hurried', which has to be RAN. Thus, if something is RANSACKED, it is rifled or, quaintly but correctly, 'given a rifle'.

By association with the above, we have

Burn bag and sack (5,4)

17

Again, the clue forces the mind to think of two containers, and someone burning them. Once again, we have 'sack' as getting the bullet, only this time, it's FIRE. We look around for synonyms for 'bag', but that puts us on a misleading track, although we're close. It isn't a physical bag, but bag in the sense of a huntsman's CATCH. CATCH FIRE thus answers 'burn'.

Here we have one that is beautiful in its symmetry, and reads with perfect sense.
Chicken and fish a problem for chef (9)
One wonders why, two simpler dishes it would be hard to find, but if a 'chicken' is a COCK, then the 'fish' is obviously ROACH, and the two are most decidedly a problem for the cook.

Staying in the kitchen, we find
Begin with Cod Surprise, to get such an effect (9)
The use of the capitals tries to suggest that there is a dish called Cod Surprise, associated with Bombe Surprise. But before you rush out to get a cook-in sauce for it, we should have a closer look. It has a very artificial appearance. Why, for instance, doesn't it say: To get such an effect, begin with Cod Surprise? That reads much more smoothly, and hasn't been used, obviously, because it is the way it is for a reason. Now, if it isn't a pure cryptic, then 'to get such an effect' has no meaning. We must go further back and try 'surprise to get such an effect'. That's much better, we can get many effects by surprise. So if that is the definition of the answer, what's left must tell us what it is. 'Begin' must be START, and an effect got by surprise has to be STARTLING. The LING is another name for 'Cod', and is a crossword favourite.

LING also doubles for heather or – more usually – the girl, Heather. She may appear, somewhat brazenly, like this,
Heather to undress in front of a young man (9)
The instructions here tell you first of all to write LING then (put) 'in front of' (it) STRIP. 'A young man' = STRIPLING.

Remembering that an 's can denote either a possessive or a shortening, an apostrophised word, therefore, is often used to deceive, as with:

Old French receiver's crime   (7)

The wording suggests crime *of* old French receiver, and inclines you to think that a specific crime is being named. All that is wrong, of course, and we must start with 'Old French', which is abbreviated to OF. A 'receiver' is a FENCE, and OFFENCE is 'crime'. What the clue actually said was 'Old French receiver is (=) crime'.

Using single letters is generally a part of the anagram scene (see *Harry or Bob about?*), but we can use various ways to suggest a single letter in non-anagram clues. For instance:

Lady teacher, 49, head of English, discharged for hurting people   (7)

Read the clue carefully for anything suspicious, to give a start. The thing that I would notice is that after all the educational build up, it doesn't finish by saying 'hurting pupils'. That suggests that the answer is going to be an object of general mayhem.

Once we have decided that, we have solved another problem. We were faced with the choice of whether 'lady teacher' or 'hurting people' was the answer definition. Now that we find pupils not mentioned, 'hurting people' must be the answer, so now we can attack the other parts of the clue to find out what the hurting thing is. 'Lady teacher' has been emphasised, rather than just teacher, so what lady teachers do we know? Governess. Headmistress. Schoolmarm. Duenna. They're no help, so go back to the happiest days of your life. What did we call them (in public)? 'It wasn't me, MISS.' So that's the first bit.

She's 49, so back to school again, to the Latin class. IL is 49, and head of *E*nglish is 'E'. That gives us MISSILE which is fired/'discharged' in war.

Notice that 'fired' would have done in the clue. After all, she had hurt people, so she must get the boot, but 'fired' would have made you think of a weapon, where 'discharged' which means exactly the same thing, suggests dismissal. The clue-maker could have used 'for hurting pupils' because missiles would hurt them as much as other people, but this would have been totally unfair. Had the answer been 'blackboard rubber' a notorious device for hurting pupils, it would be unfair to describe it as 'hurting people'. Tricks we *can* play, but deliberately misleading you on a point of definition is, in my opinion, quite outrageous.

Another device for structuring a clue is to somehow instruct you to put one word inside or outside another. With PRAWN we did it with a single letter, in this one we use a whole word:

It's in the pay of the priests   (5)

It isn't a snooper for the Inquisition, and to get it we must notice that 'it's' is short for it is. *It* is in *the*, or: T it HE = *pay*ment to the clergy.

'In the pay of' makes use of a common expression in order to deceive, and it should be mentioned at this stage that descriptions will not always be direct, or as we commonly use them, and nowhere is this more in evidence than in the 'er' words. LETTER for instance, is no longer mail, but 'one who lets' or landlord. SPANNER ceases to be a tool, and becomes a bridge. TOPPER isn't a hat any more, but a hangman.

Sometimes these can be quite oblique, as in KIPPER for one who is asleep, or SUMMER for an accountant. With this one:

A number of fingers   (5)

takes us out of the digital region, to be a 'numb-er' of fingers, which can only be FROST.

Look out for things like:

Used to drive by a sewer   (7)

First, the past tense is used to confuse, then the impression given that one is motoring past a drain. But of course, (it) is 'used'/employed by a person who sews/'sewer', and is answered by THIMBLE.

Lower animal *(3)*

suggests a rudimentary species, but it is an animal that lows, thus COW.

Two of the commonest 'er' words are FLOWER and RUNNER, both used to clue a river. BLOOMER is not a mistake (although it is, sometimes!) but a FLOWER of the garden variety. BLUBBER is a cry-baby; BUTTER a ram or goat; JUMPER a flea or frog; BANNER one who forbids something (as in 'The banner of Ancient Rome' = CENSOR) and SHOWER is one who demonstrates. There are too many to give an exhaustive list, but you'd BETTER (gambler) keep your eyes on anything the CUTTER (editor) lets through.

As with the lady teacher, we can see that Latin numerals are often brought into play to cloud our true meaning, as in:

Note a revolutionary Morris 1000 *(5)*

The word 'revolutionary' is often used to suggest an anagram, but not here, so we must take it at its face value. First, there is 'note', often an instruction to use something from the doh ray me sounds of the sol-fa system, but not so in this case, because of the shortness of the word to be found. What is immediately obvious, if it is not an anagram, is that 'Morris' is probably a proper name, and a Morris 1000 is a car – the famous MINI in fact, and the Latin notation for 1000 is M, giving MINIM, 'a note'. What is interesting about this one is that 'revolutionary Morris' is the clue for MINI; the 1000 does *not* refer to the cc. at all, but solely clues the M. This is a splendid example of the ultimate camouflage.

I have indexed all the letter group indicators at the back of the book, but I would like to emphasise the commoner ones as we go along. M is 1000, but 1000 can also be clued like this,

1000 quietly played *(5,5)*

Here you could fool around with Ms until you were black in the face, but it wouldn't help. In this we should go for the slang meaning, GRAND, so beloved of transatlantic gangsters.

'Quiet', 'quietly', 'soft' and 'softly' are all synonyms for

PIANO. PIANO is simply an abbreviation for PIANOforte, meaning soft and loud. It is, in fact, a musical direction. So PIANO as in this case, or, more usually, its shortened form P, is used to answer the words above. (Likewise F for Forte is a clue for 'loud', 'noisy' etc. Both these can be doubled to PP or FF for 'very quiet'/'loud'.) The answer GRAND PIANO has been clued as: (is) 'played'.

An example of this sort of letter indicator might be:
Blazer made of loud metallic material (5)
This conjures up an image of a 40's bookie, but in reality it is: 'Loud' = F. 'Metallic material' = LAMÉ. FLAME = 'Blazer'.

Blazer acts as a clue word for anything fiery, especially the sun.

As with IL and M, there are a large number of coded instructions for one- and two-letter groups (see LISTS) and some three-letters. It is essential that you learn the more common ones, because they are arbitrary, and cannot be worked out by any logical process.

This seeming educational comment is a good example:
Colour is a factor in educational achievement (7)
A classic! There is nothing whatsoever suspicious about it; only the fact that it's in a cryptic crossword tells you that it isn't what it seems. If we were to break it down in the traditional way: 'Colour'/'factor'/'educational' achievement, we should ruin it. It is, in fact, a more sophisticated example of the type that had 'it' in(side) 'the', but with this one, neither of the words has been given as such. You have to find what they are by deduction.

First, however, it will be useful to see what other interpretation we might put on it. It could be read as (a) 'colour' + (what) 'is a' (word for) 'factor' = 'educational achievement'. Saying that something 'is' something, or similar constructions, is a standard crossword trick. If it wasn't used, clues would lose all mystery.

When we have decided that the solution can be reached only by enclosing one word inside another, we must find out

22

what those words are. 'Colour' is the obvious synonym for the answer, so we can tackle the rest of the clue. Alternative words for 'factor' in its aspect sense as non-existent, and 'educational achievement' could be pass, diploma or degree, or it could be the letters that stand for them. These are BA, MA, DR, and DD, or, occasionally, more obscure groups. We must go back to 'factor' before we can make any further progress, and we must examine him in his commercial sense.

A 'factor' is a middleman, salesman, dealer etc. He is also an AGENT, and we can instantly put him into our academic group to get *MAGENTA*.

Here are some quickfire examples of academics in crosswords:

Graduate has a bite after cooking   (7)
Educational achievement has now become the achiever, one who has graduated from university with a degree. Here, it is BA, and he 'has a bite' or STING. 'After' (as a result of joining the two words) BASTING = 'cooking'.

Give academic a tea break   (6)
The graduate has been promoted, and is now a DON. He gets a 'tea *break*' (anagram indicator) – giving ATE. 'Give' = DONATE.

Medical man admitting it means dying of drink   (8)
Once again, the clue links a medical man with what appears to be a medical problem. There is a twist of humour here, because the definition is not totally straightforward.

'Medical man' = DR + 'admitting'/OWNING, and DROWNING is wittily described as 'dying of drink'.

Warning! 'Drink' is often a clue for SEA, from the RAF slang.

Doctor Hill's car   (5)
The doctor is now a *Medical Officer*, with a 'hill'/TOR,

23

giving MO-TOR. There are two tricks here: a false capital, and a false possessive.

Not all mention of doctors leads to medical men. Doctor can be an anagram indicator, or it could represent a general term, as here,

Not Doctor Grace getting a duck, by the sound of it (5)

Did you know W.G. Grace was a doctor? Well, he was, and therefore *not* a QUACK, which is 'the sound of a duck'. The clue was meant to deceive by suggesting that the clue was a homophone (see HOMOPHONES).

Note the use of the word 'duck' in a clue about a cricketer.

Confuse a holy man in drink (5)

Another doctor of great crossword antiquity, a doctor of divinity, or DD 'in drink', that is inserted into ALE. A dd LE = 'Confuse'.

We composers aren't short of spiritual help when it comes to our work, and we have another holy man:

Rum a holy man put on the hob (7)

A little Navy Neater's for thy stomach's sake, perhaps! Here the 'holy man' is a saint, ST, and if you put him on the 'hob'/RANGE, you get 'rum' = STRANGE.

Crosswords, I must mention here, are inadvertently male chauvinistic. We use 'man' and 'he' etc., as a matter of course. If we say 'she' then we mean something special. For your mental files, SHE answers the clue 'Haggard heroine', which is not a worn-out girl, but the woman in (Rider) Haggard's novel *She*. The same goes for 'Hardy girl', not the bulldog breed, but (Thomas) Hardy girl = TESS.

The holy man's coding also appears in this type:

Walk a little way, then catch a bus (6)

ST here is an abbreviation of street ('little way') and 'then' (+) RIDE. 'Little' or 'short', sometimes 'young', are used to indicate that a word is to be given its abbreviation. WAY is used to clue street, road, avenue etc.

24

Like Omar, we must leave doctor and saint, and go to the military.

In this one, there is a catch, and it's well worth getting the idea.

They train army boss to take pains   (7)

'Army boss' = CO; 'takes' (has added on) ACHES/'pains'. COACHES = trains.

This one is more of a problem for the solver because, unlike the other examples, if you add ACHES to CO, the resulting *sound* is of 'coaix'. When your mind runs through the possibilities, it will jump over that one, so beware. There is no way round this, except experience.

To emphasise the point, try this on some friends. Ask them what four-letter word ends in ENY. Ninety-nine per cent will say there isn't one, for the same reason as above. They will go through the alphabet, mentally testing each letter in front of the ENY sound. However, they will be pronouncing it ANY, not EE-NYE, so when they get to D it will sound like DENNY, and they will slip past DENY.

As well as army bosses and COL(onels), regiments feature strongly; as in:

Well-bred engineer punished by magistrate   (7)

The 'engineer' is an RE, sometimes clued 'sapper', and he is FINED.

Note: on the subject of fines, they can be clued as 'capital punishment', the joke reference being to capital/money.

Our engineer may meet a friend:

A couple of soldiers have a piece of cheese on toast   (7)

The RE's friend is an RA, or gunner, and they have BIT of Welsh RA-RE-BIT.

Foreign soldier takes horse to the French for a laugh   (7)

The 'foreign soldier' is always the American GI. He takes GG, the sound a child makes for 'horse' (often 'childish/kid's horse'). They go to (join up with) LE, 'the' in French, making GIGGLE.

LA, and more rarely LES, also double as 'the' in France. EL is 'the Spanish' and SI is a Spanish agreement.

Fuel for the German terror weapon (4)
hides itself very well and makes a satisfying clue, because DER is 'the' in German, 'V' were the German terror weapons, and DERV is a fuel.

Clues can be international:
In Spain, the German article is for English churchman (5)
We are not looking for the Spanish word for 'in', but 'the' in Spain = EL, and the German article (the) is DER. ELDER = 'English churchman'.

DE is 'of the French/of France', and UN or UNE, 'one of the French'. All these may be clued under the blanket definition 'continental'. UN also serves for United Nations, clued as 'World Council' or 'multinational'.

CO isn't only an army boss. It appears as 'business' or 'firm' from CO. Ltd.

Material American lawyer used to cover his face (6)
American lawyer/lawman is district attorney, DA. He has a MASK to get DAMASK, the material.

Press argument about diplomats (5)
The diplomats, from their number plates, Corps Diplomatique, CD, are put about 'argument' = ROW, for C-row-D = 'press'.

Holy man is against people playing bridge with cook (4)
The killjoy and snob is, in fact, ST for the holy man, but with ('against'/next to) people who play bridge. These are the partners east and west or north and south, as EW or NS. So,

STEW for 'cook'. NS are also 'a couple of Poles', the capital making them seem like Polish people.

A rare three-letter code is in this rather complex but exciting one:

The other way to get deputy clergyman to stand up the Sally Army   (4–5)

VICE is 'deputy', and REV(erend for clergyman). In this case he has to 'stand up' and become VER. It all then goes to the abbreviation for Sally Army, SA, to give VICE VERSA – 'the other way'.

Elizabeth Rhymer's work: 'Weather'   (5)

Don't worry if you haven't heard of the lady, she is a composite of ER for 'Elizabeth' (Regina), often clued as 'queen', and 'Rhymer's work' = ODE. (To) ERODE is (to) 'Weather'.

ER is also sometimes '(with) hesitation'.

Person who pushes a tree under trains   (5)

'Trains' are BR, and 'under' = following on, is a tree: ASH. BRASH is clued obliquely as '(like) a person who pushes/is pushy'.

My land used for party by the sea   (6)

DO is a 'party', and MAIN is crosswordese for 'sea'.

'Party' might also be CON, LAB or LIB, and SEA can be clued as 'deep' or 'drink'.

Turn Communist after getting head injury   (5)

The 'turn' doesn't mean we have to reverse anything, but indicates GO. 'Communist' is RED. 'Getting head injury' is (being) GORED.

'Communist' is also 'left', 'revolutionary' or 'extreme socialist'.

Leaving old flame mixing Gin & It.   (7)
The 'old flame' is an EX, and she takes GinIt ('mixing' is an anagram indicator), ITING. 'Leaving' is EXITING.

EX is also clued as 'former wife', 'lost love' etc.

Cheese that is shortly to be placed on trains   (4)
'That is', 'shortly'/in short, is IE, that goes 'on trains'/BR to produce the cheese, BRIE.

Public school servant is at home to fence   (5)
'Public school(boy) servant': FAG. If 'at home' one is IN, for Dickens' fence, FAGIN.

IN is also clued as 'batting' or 'playing', in its sporting sense.

Gambler pours beer all over abstainer   (6)
The 'abstainer' is teetotal or TT, with BE-tt-ER 'all over'/round.

TT is also clued as 'bike race', 'Man's race', or simply 'race'.

Avoid taking a ship on the Motorway   (4)
Ships only allowed on MAIN roads? This is a combination of two two-letter groups. SS for 'ship', on MI (M1), making MISS = 'avoid'. Note the use of I for 1. This is standard practice, as in AI for A1. It may well be that I is coded by the word 'one'.

Where we can buy cheap drink on board   (5)
makes you automatically assume we are talking about duty-free, yet the working has nothing to do with it. When we are 'on board' we are in a ship. When we realise that, we appreciate that although there is no direct instruction like 'is in', it is the same sort of clue that led us to TITHE and MAGENTA. So it boils down to 'drink in ship'. S ale S = 'where we can buy cheap'.

Since this a family book, we'll look at how the family appear in crosswords.

Father takes holy man a meal in Italy   (5)
'Father' is PA (taking) ST + A = PASTA = 'meal in Italy'. The A is placed to suggest 'a meal' but really the A follows on directly after PAST, and 'meal in Italy' stands alone.

Not to be outdone, however:

Mother takes Young Tory a bottle of wine   (5)
'Mother' is MA with CON. 'Young Tory' is a phrase, but here 'young' means short Tory/CONservative. MACON is a delicious red wine.

This is an interesting idea, very subtle:

Peculiar lord gets a game of cards   (5)
We had 'rum' for STRANGE a while back, now 'peculiar'. So: RUM + MY for card game. MY is 'lord' in the 'Good lord!' sense, and MY is equally valid for 'gosh', 'lummy', 'never', etc. More than anything we have yet seen, this clue shows how literally every aspect of day-to-day speech is used and abused by the setter.

Brother taking boatmen a cargo   (7)
A religious 'Brother' or friar = FR, taking EIGHT, a boat crew.

Tender relative   (6)
SISTER in its two meanings of nurse and 'relative'.

Vehicle (Buick 'Chief') pawnbroker described as a gem   (9)
'Vehicle' = CAR. 'Buick' (Chief letter, as in Tory leader) + pawnbroker = UNCLE, (the slang term for those useful, but much maligned functionaries). CARBUNCLE = 'a gem'.

UNCLE is also clued by 'lender' 'redeemer', 'pledgeman', etc.

Friar's fat cook   (5)
'Friar' is brother/BR, with OIL; thus 'cook' = BROIL.

It will be well worth your while to spend a few minutes reading the ONE- and TWO-LETTER GROUPS. Naturally, no one expects to know them all straight away (and I still get caught on some new ways of expressing an old idea), but the more you have hidden in that subconscious I keep harping on, the better.

TEST PAPER

a) *Chicken and pickled ostrich heads tinned   (5)*
A lot of clue for just five letters! Which two principles are in use?

b) *After a lord, one meets the Queen. No, before   (7)*
What sort of 'lord', and how is the clue broken down?

c) *Cat hair engulfs retreating foreign soldier   (7)*
A surrealistic image, indeed. It contains three ideas we've looked at. How will you go about solving it?

d) *Tells a better story than Brown or Turner   (7)*
Seemingly straightforward, but a more advanced example to have a go at. If you get this one, you're a natural, but no reason for despair if you don't.

SOLUTIONS (printed upsidedown!)

a) 'Heads' is the same as chief or leader. Heads (of) *P*ickled and *O*strich. Now, its the same as 'drinks on board'; i.e., 'tinned' is to be read as 'in a (tin) can'. Put PO in CAN to get CAPON = 'c.icken'. Note how 'Ostrich' was used to blend with chicken to suggest exotic dishes.

b) 'After a lord' (not MY!) an EARL comes. 'One' = I, 'meet' (join up with) the 'Queen' = ER, to give EARLIER.

The surnames are both misleading. 'Brown' is TAN, and goes after 'tells a better story than', which is CAPS. CAPSTAN, a device for turning, or 'Turner'. Another of the beguiling ER words. (p

The 'foreign soldier' has to be GI, and he's 'retreating': IG. 'Hair', or TRESS, 'engulfs' (goes all round) it. T-IG-RESS = 'cat'. The phrase 'Cat hair' suggested an idea, but it was totally false. (ᴐ

SOUND COMMON SENSE: Homophones

A significant number of clues will employ the 'by the sound of it' type of clue, as in:

Leather moved from side to side, by the sound of it   (5)
This requires you to think of a word for 'leather', then answer the second half of the clue 'moved from side to side' with a synonym. Here, it is SUEDE sounding like swayed.

'We hear' fulfils the same role, or:
South American country's cold, it's said   (5)
CHILE for chilly. It could be 'they/we say' or simply 'said'.

Anything that suggests that what 'is being said'/'is being heard' may conceal a homophone:
Some Royal lithographs for 'The Listener'   (6)
'Some Royal' = PRINCE, for prints = 'lithographs', 'to the ear'.

Auditor's test for bank transaction   (6)
'Auditor', strictly speaking, is a listener, as in audition, audio etc. To one who only listens, 'test' = check. CHEQUE for 'bank transaction'.

HARRY OR BOB ABOUT?
An investigation of the Anagram

SATANISM is ANTI-MASS. What good Christian could disagree with that? Yet it isn't a reassertion of fundamentalist belief, but a crossword clue that might appear like this:
Diabolical anti-mass belief! That's diabolical indeed   (8).

Clues which are anagrams (Greek for 'back letters') are *always* broken down into three parts. First, the ANAGRAM INDICATOR. This is a word or phrase which tells you that letters are to be mixed. Second, the ANAGRAM itself: a word or group of words which must be rearranged to answer the clue. And, lastly, the DEFINITION – an alternative description of the word that is the answer. Thus, in the clue above, we have the anagram indicator which is 'diabolical', and the anagram itself, 'anti-mass'. The definition is 'diabolical indeed'. The letters of the anagram are always directly in front or behind the indicator, and you have the definition to give you some help in rearranging the letters.

In this example, you will see that the same attempt as before is made to make all the parts of the clue harmonise with each other. We saw this in the two- and three-letter unit clues, but with anagrams it is generally more marked. To some extent this is done for the composer's own intellectual satisfaction, but mostly to hide the fact that it *is* an anagram.

In one sense, anagrams are the most satisfying of all the types of clue. This is because they are completely logical, and don't rely on convoluted meanings for ordinary words (not too much, anyway!). There are no flights of fancy or subtle imagery as there are with pure cryptics, and once you have identified an anagram it is a battle between you and it, man to man. However, in crosswords nothing is as simple as it seems, and we will look at some ingenious constructions that give the solver a good run for his money. (On the subject of money, if you buy a book of puzzles, you can expect to get about an hour's fun from each one. When you realise that you are getting sixty minutes of genuine pleasure for about 2p, you will realise what unparalled value they are!)

Before going into detail, there are some interesting things about the anagram that deserve a wider hearing. These days, it has the relatively humble job of entertaining us, but King James I, of Bible fame, was saved from a very sticky situation when he showed that James Stuart was an anagram of A JUST MASTER.

In even earlier times, it was part of a priest's work to predict a person's future by rearranging the letters of his name, and these 'anagram horoscopes' were considered very important.

Anagrams do seem to have something weird about them. How about HE'S TOP LETTERS MANAGER? Isn't it just a teeny bit peculiar that the same letters make THE POSTMASTER GENERAL?

Is it simply chance that SCHOOLMASTER and THE CLASSROOM have identical letters?

Obviously, the more letters you have, the easier it is to torture them into an appropriate meaning, but these are short examples, and food for thought.

As I find more and more curious anagrams, I wonder if every word contains within itself the seeds of a similar word. I have no proof, but ANGERED is an anagram of ENRAGED, and the search goes on.

The straightforward anagrams, like:

He hypnotised people into tidying up leavings   (8) (Answer: SVENGALI)

definition   =   indicator anagram

are amusing, but place intolerable limitations on the composer. As a result, it is necessary to add and subtract letters and even whole words from other words and phrases. This is much more fun for both setter and solver, and can lead to some remarkable images being conjured up. For instance:

Outrageous Page Three treat – a defecting Russian leader
(5,3,5)

A bizarre picture, indeed. However, no matter how diverting
the clue may seem, it must still work on the same principle.
Here, 'Outrageous' is the anagram indicator, 'Page Three
treat' are the letters to be mixed, and the definition is – what?
Not 'a defecting Russian leader', but just 'Russian leader'. 'A
defecting' is there to tell you that 'a' has got to be *removed*
from the anagram before it's changed. The setter could have
used 'a missing', but we all associate 'defecting' with
Russians, so the clue is given a roundness. After all that we
are left with: PETER THE GREAT.

This is the sort of clue that makes those new to cryptic
puzzles despair. Many people say to me: 'Oh, they're quite
beyond me, I haven't got the brains for that sort of thing.'
Frequently the people who say this are doing the most
complex jobs, calling for quick understanding and intuitive
grasp. I always give the same advice: try all the clues and if
you can't get some of them, work them out from the answers
the next day. Also, don't be afraid to ask advice from those
who already do puzzles. Do it for a week or so, then, hey
presto, the penny will drop, and you'll never look back. I
know it's advice that works, because it's what I did when I
started. Now I've had twenty-one books of puzzles published,
my crosswords appear all over the world, and I'm writing this
book. If I can do it, anyone can.

All you need to remember is that your daily dose of
crossword will be a source of unending pleasure for the rest of
your life. Not only that, but, if you want them to, puzzles will
open many social doors. Getting stuck on one-across would
unite a duke and a dustman like almost nothing else.

At the back of this book, there is a list of anagram
indicators. Not all of them, but every one that is in fairly
common use, and you will see that a vast number of words
and phrases can be used, as long as they imply rearrange-
ment, chaos or interference. Words like 'change', 'order',
'arrange' and 'sort' are fairly obvious; while 'trouble', 'variety'
and 'free' are less immediately recognisable, and 'butcher',
'doctor' and 'curious' need experience. Frequently, the

indicator will be a phrase like 'at 6s and 7s', or 'all over the place', and the varieties are endless, so you will need to understand the principle, rather than refer to a list.

I must stress again, wherever possible the anagram indicator will try to merge so well with the rest of the clue that it no longer seems to be an anagram, as in:
Harry Worth to get the chuck? (5)
On the face of it, a nice TV personality is threatened with the sack. If you hadn't realised that 'Harry' was an indicator, meaning to ravage and destroy, you would have been up a gum tree. The only inkling you might have got is that there seems very little information if the clue *isn't* an anagram. However, we've seen clues shorter than that, so an anagram wasn't certain. Anyway, if we 'harry'/destroy 'Worth' we get THROW = 'chuck'.

Constant vigilance is necessary if you are not to waste time on clues that are anagrams, imagining them to be two- or three-unit clues. Ideally, you ought to read each clue as a possible anagram until your 'solver's nose' comes fully into play.
    Which of these two strikes you as an anagram, and which not?
Marshal Ney's aunt's an Oriental leader   (3,3–3) or
St Peter, if upset, goes after US general   (9)
There seems to be no indicator for the first one, although 'upset' would seem to an indicator for the second. This impression is strengthened by the fact that there are nine letters immediately in front of it, suggesting that it is an anagram of ST PETER IF. Surprisingly, the reverse turns out to be true. In the first example, 'Marshal', meaning 'to arrange in order' is the anagram indicator for 'Ney's aunts', giving us the Chinese leader, SUN YAT-SEN.
    The second clue, is not an anagram at all. 'Upset' refers only to 'if' becoming FI. We then put an American general, SHERMAN on it, to get 'St Peter' = FISHERMAN.

As we saw with 'a defecting', the more complex anagrams call for the removal of one or more letters, as in,

A Tandoori curry: love a duck, when gone it leaves us glowing (7)

It sounds like another satisfied customer down at the Star of India, doesn't it? However, if we look at it more closely we can't help noticing the very artificial way the ideas are expressed. Why, for instance, does it say 'when gone', not 'when *it's* gone'? Of course, it *is* an anagram, but it needs some more work done on it. 'Curry' is the obvious indicator, yet we have two groups of nine letters on either side. The 'when gone' must be playing the 'defecting' role, in which case what has got to be removed, and from where? 'Love a duck' is so obviously contrived, that it must hold the answer. Let us split them, to avoid the Cockney impression it's desperate to create. We then have DUCK and LOVE, very similar to CUT and RUN, and SPIDER and FLY which we had earlier. It will dawn on us, sooner or later, that DUCK and LOVE both stand for nil in their respective sports. So we have OO to remove from 'Tandoori'; when we do 'it leaves us (the solvers)' with ATANDRI, 'curried', which is RADIANT = 'glowing'.

Now, just when we seemed to have reached a haven of stability in a rocking world, we have:
If the lamb curry is off, dismiss restaurant's chief meat supplier (6, 7)

It doesn't look as if 'curry' is the indicator here, because there aren't enough useful letters on either side of it. So, is there another candidate? 'Off' or 'is off' suggest themselves, and 'is off' could tell us that 'if the lamb curry' contains the letters we want. But that has fourteen letters, so we must lose one. Here, it seems that 'dismiss' is doing 'defecting's' job, and that '*r*estaurant's chief' must be removed. That leaves 'if the lamb cury' to yield a 'meat supplier'. Sorted through, we find that we have FAMILY BUTCHER.

Keep your eyes peeled for words like 'chief', 'head (of)', 'leader' and 'top'. Often they will tell you that only the initial letter is to be used or removed. *C*harles the First, *F*irst Lieutenant, Head of the *h*ouse, Top of the *s*hop, or *B*andleader.

On the same principle, other letter positions can be indicated. Henry the Second. Richard the Third. Likewise, Close of play, Last of the Mohicans and the End of the affair. Take care, Elmer's End is R, not S. Tory leader is, appositely, T.

On the subject of removing letters, someone once said to Lord Macaulay: 'If I make an anagram of Napoleon's name, and miss out the E, I can make the name of the Beast in Revelations.' Macaulay, who didn't suffer fools gladly, put the man down with this marvellous squelch. 'Who, Sir, are *you*' he replied, 'to leave out an E?' It is nonetheless interesting that anagrams were still thought significant in the nineteenth century.

Now try
French author's translation of Molière's 'Eliza' has rise taken out of it (5,4)
On the face of it, a literary clue of no small difficulty. However, 'translation of' would seem to be the indicator for Molière's Eliza with 'rise' taken out of it. If we then juggle the remaining letters, we get the French author, EMILE ZOLA.

Just one more to emphasise how the blending of anagram, indicator and definition should create a cohesive whole:
Impious doctor is struck off for supplying drug addicts (5)
That is a nice clue; it all ties in beautifully. The thing that should make you suspicious is 'Impious'. When you think of all the words there are available to describe a criminal doctor: dastardly, felonious etc., it is funny that a word with religious overtones has been chosen. The 'doctor', a traditional anagram word, lends credence to the fact that the word hides our answer. Before that, however, we are told that 'is struck off', so we remove IS from 'impious', 'doctor' it, and come up with OPIUM. With 'doctor', 'struck off' and 'drug addict' in the clue, its camouflage was almost perfect.

Other anagrams will need words or letters adding to them, as:
A terrible crime, taking a country that doesn't belong to us (7)

40

Indeed it is, but this isn't simply an anti-imperialist statement, but a complex mixture of letters. It resolves itself like this:

A *terrible*   *crime*   a *country not ours*
   indicator   anagram   definition
 A   MERIC   A = AMERICA

The 'As' are already supplied, and the clue progresses logically, but those 'As' merge with the other words to hide the fact that they must be used separately.

Hill retires to rest after turning out nasty fellows   (7)
Once again, there is the suggestion of a person. However, 'Hill' is TOR retiring, ROT; 'to' (joining) 'rest' (anagram) 'after' (when) there has been a 'turning out'. So, add TERS to make ROTTERS.

Do keep on the alert. Anagram indicators will always be made to harmonise with the anagram and the definition, so they will escape detection if you aren't ever vigilant. What about
Old Nick's schedule D income   (7)?
'Schedule D' and 'income' may well so put your mind in handcuffs that you reject the idea of an anagram. 'Schedule' is defined as 'arrange', and 'Income D' = DEMONIC = 'Old Nick *is*'. Not a possessive, you see.

Revoke cat licence for duck   (4,5)
Another surrealistic clue. 'Licence' is defined as 'deviation from form' or 'wildness', both obvious indicators. 'Revoke cat' yields up TAKE COVER, or another sort of 'duck'.
   'Free' is a commoner variety of the 'licence' concept, with 'Liberal(ly)' also in use.

Some anagrams are true works of art, and I would like you to appreciate just how ingenious and self-contained they can be.
'Nascent' is translated as 'Starting', not 'Stopping'   (9)

Now, 'Nascent' *does* meaning 'Starting'. Obviously, therefore, it can't mean 'Stopping'. So far, the clue is a somewhat heavy-handed statement of fact. 'Translated' we've met before as an anagram indicator, and since 'Nascent' is an English word, it isn't strictly appropriate. 'Defined' would have been more reasonable. So, it's an anagram of 'Nascent is', but to define what? With all the capitals, commas and inverted commas, the true definition has been almost totally hidden.

If it were to be written: starting (and) not stopping, then 'nascent is' could give us INCESSANT.

As with other clues, the substitution of letters for numbers is the same:
He gets 11 per cent off (9)
Discount that clue? 11 is II + per cent. Off is the indicator. Answer: RECIPIENT = 'he gets'. Note the male usage, as mentioned earlier. 'He' is thought of as anybody, 'she' makes us think of a specific person or type.

Captials, added or omitted, play their parts well:
Change at Naples for Nice (8)
is a round sort of clue, with implications of EEC air travel. But 'change' (indicator) 'at naples' which becomes PLEASANT to answer the definition 'nice', not 'Nice'.

A look at the one- and two-letter group lists will give you more ammunition.

TEST PAPER

a) *In the list below, what word is* not *an indicator?*
MINCE, MASH, MARINATE, CURRY, STEW, MINCE.

b) *In this list, which is the indicator?*
PLATE, SAUCER, POT, DISH, TUREEN, SALVER.

c) *This is from a puzzle I set for a charity magazine; can you get the answer and understand the working?*
Charity's quit by Sir Bob. That's crafty! (5)

d) *In this one, which is the indicator, the anagram and the definition?*
Lunatic or manic Italian   (7)

e) *A tricky one, this! 'Doctor' is obviously the indicator, but which is the anagram, and which the definition, as there are thirteen letters on either side of 'doctor'?*
Luther drowned Doctor Faustus in this   (3,10)

f) *Can you work out what on earth is going on here?*
Calling to see drunken man with gin cocktail   (6)

g) *A new trick, can you spot it?*
Warlike order detailed Armalite   (7)

SOLUTIONS (printed upsidedown!)

a) MARINATE. All the other suggest mixing or cutting.

b) DISH. It means to upset or overturn.

c) 'Sir' quits 'Chartys', leaving CHATY. 'Bob' is indicator (i.e. to bob about). 'That's crafty' is a pun on 'like a craft or YACHT.

d) 'Lunatic' is the indicator, 'or manic' the anagram and 'Italian' the definition; with the result, MARCONI. This is quite difficult because it could have been 'Lunatic' (definition) 'or' (=), 'Manic' (indicator) and 'Italian' (anagram).

e) The key to this one was to realise that, on its own, 'Luther drowned' couldn't mean anything, whereas 'Faustus in this' could. It is an anagram of THE UNDERWORLD.

f) Two anagrams for the price of one. 'Man' ('drunken' indicator) and 'gin' ('cocktail' indicator). NAM + ING. When you solve it, you 'see' the answer.

g) 'Armalite' is 'detailed' (tail taken off), when ordered (indicator). ARMALIT = MARTIAL = 'warlike'.

A LITTLE OF WHAT YOU FANCY!
The cryptic clue

With the cryptic clue, it would not be too much to say that 'a way with words' has reached its highest peak. Great novelists are rightly praised for the brilliance of their prose, but the crossword composer's ability to fancifully, but fairly, describe a word or phrase in a short, cunning and humorous way is rarely accorded the same attention.

Cryptic clues have a lot in common with puns. Unlike all the other types we've seen, they are not made up of units, nor do they contain any instructions, as such. They are simply a way of saying something that is ... well, cryptic! Let's have a look at some.

Drawing of Hoover (7)
A sketch of the depression president? No, it's the other Hoover, not J Edgar, although they both had a hand in removing dirt: Mr (vacuum cleaner) Hoover. Now light dawns! This is not a picture, but the SUCTION of *a* hoover. It is always surprising to observe how some things swell up to eclipse all others. Hoover is now 'vacuum cleaner', not a trade name. I once heard someone ask for an Electrolux hoover.

Where one doesn't expect to be found guilty of a crime (7)
Use of the phrase 'to be found guilty' automatically makes one think of a court, and a lenient one in this case. However, what the clue is really saying is, 'if guilty of a crime, where you might expect not to be found'; i.e., where a guilty person goes

to ground. HIDEOUT fits the bill nicely.

The storm breaks   (5)
That seems to be saying 'the storm starts'. Certainly, 'breaks'
does mean 'begins', but it also means 'let-ups', and there is the
route to the right answer, LULLS.

Likewise with:
Breaks under torture   (8)
It isn't 'to break' as suggested by the way it's laid out, but 'let-
ups' again, this time RESPITES.

Although cryptics are using words with unconnected
meanings in a situation that seems to have a connection, with
them you have no instructions. There are no indicators, no
suggestions that one word should be 'in' another, and no
logical progression of steps. The 'solver's nose' is nowhere
more needed, but it does help if you constantly look for
alternative meanings to the main ideas in a cryptic clue:

Goes to bed in the hope of getting up   (7)
Because it says 'bed' and 'getting up' doesn't automatically
mean that either of them have anything to do with sleep.
What other sorts of bed are there? Flower bed comes to mind
immediately. Now, 'up' takes on a new significance. Flowers
come 'up', so the answer must be 'what we do if we go to a
(flower) bed, with the hope (aim) of getting (flowers) up'. We
might dig or hoe, but the blanket term is 'to garden', and
GARDENS is the answer.

This is an interesting one,
Produced very little crackling, having stolen pig, perhaps (7)
Pork crackling comes deliciously to mind, but isn't any help.

'Produced very little crackling' might hint at 'didn't make
much noise', and we should keep that in mind. The 'perhaps'
is there to tell us that it could be a pig, but doesn't have to be.
From that we might deduce that any stolen animal would do.
If so, then we want a generic word for 'having stolen pig'. The

first thing to do is to sort out the right tense. It isn't 'having' in the possessive, but 'having stolen'. Thus 'having stolen (animal)' could well be RUSTLED, and must be, because it so perfectly answers the first half of the clue.

With,
The Government funds his area of study   (9)
we appear to have a lucky scientist. However, 'funds' isn't a verb, and 'Government funds' must be read as 'the money that belongs to the state' is 'studied by him'. After that, he can be nothing but an ECONOMIST.

The length of the Bible?   (5)
must bring back memories of the vastness of the book, as indeed it is meant to. But what we are asking really is, give us the name of the measurement of length mentioned *in* the Bible.

Put like that, CUBIT immediately springs to mind.

Close eyes to counter this vision problem?   (4,5)
suggests *closing* the eyes, in pain perhaps. Not a bit of it, 'Close' in the sense of 'near', and by putting your eyes close, you will eliminate the problem of NEAR SIGHT.

Council house charges   (5)
Council house is such a strong image, that it will hold you up for ever if you don't get it into shape. 'House charges' (of/by) 'council' = RATES. RATES are never paid, as such, on council houses, only private ones, but with 'Council house' written down, it has an almost mesmeric effect.

Cryptic clues are all about misplaced emphasis, to a degree rarely experienced with other types of clue. Never take the lift the composer offers you, as – in real life – once you go along with him, you are likely to come to a sticky end! As in:
Undressing skittishly?   (6,3)

47

suggesting a low-key striptease. 'Skittishly' looks the more hopeful of the two words, so we should look at it more closely. It means 'in a mildly wanton manner' which is little help. It comes from the word 'skit', and in that we think of satire. Skits are often lampoons, where people are subjected to gentle ridicule. A synonym would be 'a take off'. That gels nicely with 'undressing' to make TAKING OFF the answer. The question mark told you that a broad interpretation of the words was going to be called for. That meant that we should read 'in the manner of a skit' for 'skittish'.

Powered flight (9)

isn't hard, once the Wright Brothers' image goes. We can then look at other meanings of 'flight' such as 'escape' or 'stairs' Powered stairs gives us ESCALATOR.

Isn't a sportsman defeated? (3,5)

The question mark is there to take your mind away from 'isn't' and make you just take it for granted. 'Sportsman defeated' seems to be where the bulk of the clue lies, but that isn't so. Read it like this: 'Is not a sportsman (when) defeated.' That can be nothing else but BAD LOSER.

Keep a stern eye on question marks, they aren't what they seem. In cryptics, punctuation is still used fraudulently.

Public Enemy No. 1? Hardly! (5,8)

The clue is asking if a person is a major criminal, then implying he most certainly isn't. Now the answer is going to be either a saint, or a criminal very unlikely to be thought of as a serious menace. 'No. 1' is 'chief' (some hope there), or 'first'. A 'public enemy', stricly, is *anybody* who has broken the law – only in popular films has he become the monster he is. So 'offender' will do. A FIRST OFFENDER is traditionally thought of as a trifling sort of criminal, therefore 'hardly' a true 'Public Enemy No. 1'.

You can see, by now, that it is really all down to your intuition, helped along by the ability to look at the clue in any light except the one the composer obviously wants you to. Attack *what is written down in cold print,* ignore what the clue seems to say.

Receiver employed by Oriental solicitor   (7,4)
Two law men. True, a solicitor *may* employ a receiver, but not here. Solicitors are, also, people who solicit things. A thing solicited, particularly in the East, is alms. And what do solicitors of alms traditionally have in the East to 'receive' the money? BEGGING BOWL.

Cleanse each clue of the camouflage paint you *know* has been put on it. Trust nothing. Not a capital, full stop or question mark.

An 'Excuse-me' at the Palais?   (5,6)
I won't ask if you come here often, but 'Excuse me' and 'Palais' are too good to be true. They are the only two possible elements that can have any bearing on the answer. Another word for 'excuse-me' is PARDON. What has been done to 'Palais', if anything? Well, it was probably 'palace', Frenchified to tie in with 'excuse me'. That's no longer necessary, so 'palace' it is. Who lives in a palace? Royalty. So ROYAL PARDON, is the witty answer to a faultless clue from a technical point of view.

As is this one:
Place for person who has a complaint to lay   (4-3)
It is hard to resist the idea of a moan, and one thinks of a suggestion box or Trading Standards Office. But 'complaint' is also illness, and where one with an illness will lie is a SICK-BED. The idea conveyed by 'a complaint to lay' as one unit was overwhelming, but we were deceived; it was 'where to lay with a complaint' after all.

Auto-wrecking in Japan   (4–4)
'Auto-wrecking' *has* to make you think of a breaker's yard in Old Nippon? Not right! 'Auto' in the sense of auto-suggestion, i.e., 'self'. 'Self-wrecking' is suicide, which is HARI-KIRI in Japan.

A last example finally to dispel any idea that a clue should even be *thought about* in its original state.
Make yourself a late supper   (4,3,6)
That can only be 'cook a snack before bed' if there is any justice left in the world! But no: here 'late' means 'no longer', as in 'gunner Jones, late of the guards'. 'Supper' is an ER word, one who sups, or drinks. Therefore: 'Make yourself no longer a boozer' must be SIGN THE PLEDGE.

That concludes our jaunt through the magic of crosswords. I hope you'll go on to enjoy fully the delights cryptic clues have in store for you. From me, it is not farewell, we have many trysts to keep: in early morning trains, high flying aircraft, and at home on a wet Sunday.

TEST PAPER

a) *Fair competition   (6,7)*
The good business impression misleads; which one of the words would you analyse first?

b) *Tooting man held responsible for abducting children (3,4,5)*
A South London criminal, or what...?

c) *One with volume control always set on 'quiet'   (9)*
A considerate HiFi fan, or do you have a better idea?

d) *Ideal for a deep sleep?   (7)*
That could be so many things, a cryptic as pure as the driven snow. What do you think is the key word?

SOLUTIONS (printed upsidedown!)

a) The word to concentrate on was 'fair', it has so many synonyms and words that are both homophones and homonyms. The answer lies in reading 'fair' in the sense of lovely, so you could arrive at BEAUTY CONTEST.

b) Obviously, then, it's THE PIED PIPER. Not the area, but 'tooting' on a musical instrument.

c) 'Volume control' (one who has it) is a LIBRARIAN, a group noted for their obsession with silence; i.e., they're 'set' on it.

d) The key word was 'deep'. It's 'deep' in the sea sense, so, for a sleep at sea/on a ship, traditionally, a HAMMOCK.

NOTES ON USING THE LISTS

Before you try to digest the contents, I think you ought to know some of the general principles crossword composers work on. There should never be an attempt to use specialised knowledge, obscure references to books of fact or fiction, or to people and things outside the normal scope of a person who has read a reasonable cross section of books and magazines. The puzzle should fit the man on the Clapham omnibus, as long as he sometimes catches it to go to the library.

Examples are always the best way to describe something, so I would expect you to know that wolfram was the old name for tungsten, but not which metals went to make up Pinchbeck (copper and a soupçon of zinc!). I will assume a casual acquaintanceship with the premier Deities of Greece, Rome, Egypt and the Vikings, but I'll take for granted an ignorance approaching my own on creatures worshipped elsewhere.

This leads on to the LISTS. They are not there as a work of reference, but I intend them to jog your memory, and to this end I have tried to put in as much information as I can, particularly knowledge of the kind that you can find nowhere else. Thus, you can find the names of the seven Dwarfs, the astronauts on the Apollo moonshot, and a list of slang terms for money, all under one cover. I have cross-referenced the alphabetical index, but the lists themselves are in random order. Not that they are truly random because, and I can't explain it, there are 'intuitive' links between various groups. As you will discover in the text, crossword clues rely a great deal on using words that have two dissimilar meanings. So, if you read through the DANCES, you find GIG cross referenced to SHIPS, and so on. You'll also, I hope, just browse through them for amusement, and I expect you will find them as fascinating to read as I did when I wrote them.

The sub lists, those that deal with the words used to indicate anagrams, and the many abbreviations we use, are self-explanatory, once you have read the book.

LISTS

Inns of Court

Inner Temple   Middle Temple   Gray's Inn   Lincoln's Inn

Artificial Languages

There are more than 500 invented languages, and over 300 computer languages. This is a very small selection of the most famous:

INVENTED LANGUAGES – Esperanto, Idiom Neutral, Interglossa, Interlingua, Novial, Occidental, Pankel, Tutonish, Volapuk.

COMPUTER LANGUAGES – Algol, (*see* STARS) Basic, Cobol, Fortran, List, Modula, Pascal, Prologue.

Roman Roads

Ermine Street   Fosse Way   Watling Street

Monks

Acoumeti	Black	Cistercian	Grey
Augustinian or	Capuchin	Crutched	Trappist
Austin	Carmelite	Culdee	White
Basilian	Carthusian	Dominican	
Benedictine	Celestine	Franciscan	
(*see* ALCOHOL)			

Winds

The classical winds – Aquilon, Auster, Boreas,
Eurus, Favonius, Libeccio, Natus, Zephyr.
Wind types – cyclone, hurricane, typhoon, dustdevil,
tornado, waterspout.
Regional winds: mistral, monsoon, sirocco.

Judges

Lord Chancellor, Lord Chief Justice, Master of the
Rolls, Common Serjeant, recorder (*see* MUSICAL
INSTRUMENTS), referee, master.

The Rare Gases

Argon, helium, krypton, neon, radon, xenon.

Royal Residences

Buckingham Palace, Clarence House, Glamis Castle,
Hampton Court, Holyrood House, Osborne House,
Windsor Castle.

Virtues

PLATO: justice, prudence, temperance, fortitude.
CHRISTIAN: faith, hope, charity.

Chinese Years

rat	cat	horse	rooster
buffalo	dragon	goat	dog
tiger	snake	monkey	pig

The Seven Sisters

Alcoyne, Asterope, Celaeno, Electra, Maia, Merope, Taygeta.

Medals and Decorations

Africa Star
Albert Medal
Atlantic Star
Bath, order of
British Empire Medal
British Empire, order of
Burma Star
Distinguished Flying Cross/
   Medal
Distinguished Service Cross/
   Medal
Garter, order of
George Cross/Medal
Honour, Companion of
Merit, order of
Military Cross/Medal
St Michael & George, order of
St Patrick, order of
Victoria Cross
Victorian Order, Royal

Ways to Cook

bake
baste
boil
braise
broil

casserole
chip
curry
fricassé
fry

grill
poach
roast
scald
scramble

simmer
steam
toast

Beaufort Scale

calm air
light air
light breeze

gentle breeze
moderate breeze
fresh breeze

strong breeze
moderate gale
fresh gale

strong gale
storm
violent storm

hurricane (*see* WINDS)

Dickens' Novels

Barnaby Rudge
Bleak House
Chimes
Christmas Carol
Cricket on the Hearth
David Copperfield
Dombey and Son
Great Expectations
Hard Times
Little Dorrit

Martin Chuzzlewit
Mystery of Edwin Drood
Nicholas Nickleby
Oliver Twist
Old Curiosity Shop
Our Mutual Friend
Pickwick Papers
Tale of Two Cities
Uncommercial Traveller

Horse Parts

cannon	flank	hoof	poll
coronet	gaskin	loin	stifle
croupe	haunch	mane	throatlatch
fetlock	hock	pastern	withers
forelock			

Rivers of Hell

Acheron Cocytus Phlegethon Styx

Dewey Decimal System

The classifications into which all non-fiction is divided.

fine arts	literature	philosophy	useful arts/applied
general works	natural science	religion	science
history	philology	sociology	

Shaw's Plays

His best known works are:

Androcles and the Lion
Arms and the Man
Apple Cart
Back to Methuselah
Caesar and Cleopatra
Candida
Captain Brassbound's
   Conversion
Devil's Disciple
Don Juan in Hell
Dark Lady of the Sonnets
Doctor's Dilemma

In Good King Charles's Golden
   Days
Heartbreak House
John Bull's other Island
Man and Superman
Millionairess
Misalliance
Pygmalion
Philanderer
Saint Joan
Too True to be Good
Village Wooing

Cricket Positions

deep fine leg	midwicket	long off	cover point
short fine leg	long on	mid on	gulley
long leg	short square leg	mid off	slips
square leg	silly mid on	extra cover	third man

Brontës

Anne (Pseudonym: Acton Bell), Charlotte (Currer Bell)
Emily (Ellis Bell), Bramwell, their brother, Reverend Patrick,
father.
Their most famous novels are:– Anne: *The Tenant of Wildfell Hall*, Charlotte: *Jane Eyre* and Emily: *Wuthering Heights*.

Vessels

argo (*see* ARGO)
barge
bark
bâteau
battleship
berthon
bilander
bireme
brig (antine)
bumboat
buss
canoe
caravel
carrach/k
catamaran
catboat
clipper
coaster
coble
collier
coracle
corvette
crimster
cruiser
cutter
destroyer

dhow
dinghy
dory (*see* FISH)
dreadnought
dredger
drifter
dromond
dugout
eight
felucca
ferry
fireship
foist
frigate
funny
galleon
galley
galliot
gallivat
gig (*see* DANCES)
gondola
grab
hopper
houseboat
hoy
icebreaker

indiaman
jangrada
jollyboat
junk
katamaran
kayak
ketch
launch
levanter
lifeboat
lighter
lightship
liner
longboat
lugger
motorboat
motorlaunch
nuggar
outrigger
packet
paddlesteamer
pinnace
piragua
polacca
punt
randan

razee
sampan
schooner
sculler
sealer
shell
showboat
skiff
slaver
sloop
snow
speedboat
submarine
tanker
tender
tramp
trawler
trow
tub
tug
umiac
whaler
windjammer
yacht
yawl
xebec

Elements

actinium (Ac)
aluminium (Al)
americium (Am)
antimony (Sb)
argon (Ar)
arsenic (As)
astatine (At)
barium (Ba)
berkelium (Bk)
beryllium (Be)
bismuth (Bi)
boron (B)
bromine (Br)
cadmium (Cd)
calcium (Ca)
californium (Cf)
carbon (C)
cerium (Ce)
caesium (Cs)
chlorine (Cl)
chromium (Cr)
cobalt (Co)
columbium (Cb)
copper (Cu)
curium (Cm)
dysprosium (Dy)
einsteinium (Es)
erbium (Er)
europium (Eu)
fermium (Fm)
flourine (F)
francium (Fr)
gadolinium (Gd)
gallium (Ga)
germanium (Ge)

gold (Au)
Hafnium (Hf)
helium (He)
holmium (Ho)
hydrogen (H)
indium (Im)
iodine (I)
iridium (Ir)
iron (Fe)
krypton (Kr)
lanthanum (La)
lawrencium (Lr)
lead (Pb)
lithium (Li)
lutetium (Lu)
magnesium (Mg)
manganese (Mn)
mendelevium (Md)
mercury (Hg)
molybdenum (Mo)
neodymium (Nd)
neon (Ne)
neptunium (Np)
nickel (Ni)
niobium (Nb)
nitrogen (N)
nobellium (No)
osmium (Os)
oxygen (O)
palladium (Pd)
phospherous (P)
platinum (Pt)
plutonium (Pu)
polonium (Po)
potassium (K)

praseodymium (Pr)
promethium (Pm)
protactinium (Pa)
radium (Ra)
radon (Rn)
rhenium (Re)
rhodium (Rh)
rubidium (Rb)
ruthenium (Ru)
samarium (Sm)
scandium (Sc)
selenium (Se)
silicon (Si)
silver (Ag)
sodium (Na)
strontium (Sr)
sulphur (S)
tantalum (Ta)
technetium (Tc)
tellurium (Te)
terbium (Tb)
thallium (Tl)
thorium (Th)
thulium (Tm)
tin (Sn)
titanium (Ti)
tungsten (W)
uranium (U)
vanadium (V)
wolfram (W)
xenon (Xe)
ytterbium (Yb)
yttrium (Y)
zinc (Zn)
zirconium (Zr)

Gangsters

camorra	firm	mob	tong
cosa nostra	mafia	syndicate	triad

Canadian Provinces

Alberta	Newfoundland	Ontario
British Columbia	New South Wales	Prince Edward Island
Manitoba	North West Territories	Quebec
New Brunswick	Nova Scotia	Yukon

Sub-Atomic Particles

baryon	lepton	parton	quark
electron	meson	photon	thermion
fermion	muon	pion	
hadron	neutron	positron	
kaon	neutrino	proton	

Law Sittings

Hilary	Easter	Trinity	Michaelmas

Greek Alphabet

alpha	eta	nu	tau
beta	theta	xi	upsilon
gamma	iota	omicron	phi
delta	kappa	pi	chi
epsilon	lambda	rho	psi
zeta	mu	sigma	omega

Seven Ages of Man

Infant, schoolboy, lover, soldier, justice, old age, second childhood.

French Revolutionary Calendar

Jan:	PLUVIOSE (rain)	Jul:	THERMIDOR (heat)
Feb:	VENTOSE (wind)		FERVIDOR (heat)
Mar:	GERMINAL (seed)	Aug:	FRUCTIDOR (fruit)
Apr:	FLOREAL (blossom)	Sep:	VENDEMIERE (vintage)
May:	PRAIRAL (pasture)	Oct:	BRUMAIRE (fog)
Jun:	MESSIDORE (harvest)	Nov:	FRIMAIRE (sleet)
		Dec:	NIVOSE (snow)

Thus thirteen months of twenty-eight days each.

Canonical Hours
(In natural order)
Matins, lauds, prime, terce, sext, none, vespers, compline.

The Muses

Calliope: epic poetry	Melpomene: tragedy	Terpsichore: dance
Cleo: history	Thalia: comedy	Polyhymnia: hymns
Euterpe: lyric poetry	Erato: erotic poetry	Urania: astronomy

Seven Wonders of the World

Great Pyramid	Mausoleum at Halicarnassus
Hanging Gardens of Babylon	Colossus at Rhodes
Statue of Zeus at Olympia	Pharos Lighthouse at Alexandria
Temple of Diana at Ephesus	

Geological Ages

Precambrian	Devonian	Jurassic	Miocene
Cambrian	Carboniferous	Cretaceous	Pliocene
Ordovician	Permian	Eocene	Pleistocene
Silurian	Triassic	Oligocene	

Present day: Holocene

Phonetic Signs
(Diacritics)

Accent, breve, cedilla, circumflex, diaresis, hacek, macron, tilde, trema, umlaut.

Seven Dwarfs

Bashful, Doc, Dopey, Grumpy, Happy, Sleepy, Sneezy.

Paris, Judgement of

A golden apple, marked 'For the Fairest', was claimed by ATHENA, HERA and APHRODITE. Awarded to Aphrodite by PARIS. His reward was help from Aphrodite in kidnapping HELEN. This caused the losers to conspire, and bring about the TROJAN war.

Twelve Apostles

Simon, called Peter	Thomas
Andrew, his brother	Matthew, the tax collector
James, son of Zebedee	James, son of Alpheus
and his brother John	Thaddeus
Philip	Simon of Cannae
Bartholomew	Judas Iscariot

Cabal

Meaning any powerful group operating in secret. From the initial letters of the group in Charles the Second's government:
Clifford, Arlington, Buckingham, Ashley, Lauderdale.

Champagne

The sizes of Champagne bottles, in ascending order, are:
magnum, jeroboam, rehoboam, methuselah, salmanazar, belshazzar, nebuchadnezzar.

Argo
(principal crew)

Jason, Heracles, Orpheus, Castor, Polydeuces, Echion, Idas, Lynceus.

Police Ranks

constable	chief inspector	commander
sergeant	superintendent	assistant commissioner
inspector	chief superintendent	commissioner

Four Horsemen of Apocalypse

As mentioned in the Revelations of St John: War, Famine, Pestilence and Death (The Pale Horseman).

Seven Against Thebes

Tydeus, Capaneus, Hippomedon, Parthenopaeus, Amphiarchus, Polynices, Etioclus.

Three Musketeers

Aramis Athos Porthos   Leader: D'Artagnan

Old Testament

Genesis	Kings 1 and 2	Song of Solomon	Obadiah
Exodus	Chronicles 1	Isaiah	Jonah
Leviticus	and 2	Jeremiah	Micah
Numbers	Ezra	Lamentations	Nahum
Deuteronomy	Nehemiah	Ezekial	Habakkuk
Joshua	Esther	Daniel	Zephaniah
Judges	Job	Hosea	Haggai
Ruth	Psalms	Joel	Zachariah
Samuel 1	Proverbs	Amos	Malachi
and 2	Ecclessiates		

New Testament

Matthew	Corinthians	Timothy	Peter
Mark	Galatians	Titus	John
Luke	Ephesians	Philemon	Jude
John	Philippians	Hebrews	Revelations
Acts	Colossians	Epistles of:	
Epistles to:	Thessalonians	James	
Romans			

Apocrypha

Esdras	Ecclesiasticus	History of Susanna
Tobit	Baruch	Bel and the Dragon
Judith	Jeremy	Prayer of Manasses
Esther	Song of Holy	Maccabees
Wisdom of Solomon	Children	Enoch

66

Livery Companies
(twelve senior)

mercers	fishmongers	merchant taylors	ironmongers
grocers	goldsmiths	haberdashers	vintners
drapers	skinners	salters	clothworkers

Sacred Robes

alb	cotta	maniple	sircingle
amice	crozier	(*see* ROMAN LEGION)	soutane
biretta	dalmatic	mitre	stock
cassock	fanon	omophorion	stole
chasuble	lappet	pallium	tunicle

Plant Parts

anther	cyme	petal	style
bract	filament	pistil	raceme
capitulum	ovary	sepal	umbel
carpel	panicle	stamen	
corymb	pedicel	stigma	

Seven Deadly Sins

Anger, covetousness, envy, gluttony, lust, pride, sloth.

Musical Instruments
(a selection)

accordion	concertina	jew's harp	sitar
alpenhorn	cornet	kazoo	sousaphone
bagpipes	cymbals	kettledrum	spinet
balalaika	double bass	lute	tambourine
banjo	drum	lyre	timbrel
bassoon	dulcimer	mandoline	triangle
bass	english horn	oboe	trombone
bouziki	euphonium	ocarina	trumpet
bugle	french horn	panpipe	tuba
castanets	fugelhorn	piano	ukulele
cello	glockenspiel	piccolo	violin
cembalo	guitar	recorder	violoncello
cithera	harmonica	sackbut	vibraphone
clarion	harpsichord	saxophone	xylophone
clavichord	hecklephone	sistrum	zither

Atmosphere

Lithosphere (ground), trophosphere, stratosphere, mesosphere, ionosphere, exosphere.

Gilbert & Sullivan

Thespis	HMS Pinafore	Mikado
Trial by Jury	Ruddigore	Yeomen of the Guard
Sorcerer	Peer and Peri	Gondoliers
Patience	Princess Ida	Utopia Ltd
Pirates of Penzance	Castle Adamant	Grand Duke

Fish

anchovy
angelfish
bass
barbel
barnacle
barracuda
blenny
bloater
bream
brill
brisling
burbot
carp
catfish
chad
char
chubb
clam
cockle
cod
codling
coelacanth
conger
crab
crayfish
cuttlefish
dab
dace

doctor
dogfish
dory
dugong
eel
flatfish
flounder
gar
garfish
goldfish
grayling
grouper
gudgeon
guppy
haddock
hake
halibut
herring
jellyfish
kipper
lamprey
launce
ling
lobster
luce
mackerel
manatee
meagre

medusa
merling
minnow
moray
morgay
mullet
mussel
octopus
oyster
parr
perch
pike
pilchard
plaice
pollack
porgy
prawn
ray
red-eye
roach
rudd
salmon
sardine
shad
shark
shrimp
skate
smelt

snapper
snoek
sole
sparling
sprat
squid
stingaree
stingray
stockfish
sturgeon
swordfish
tarpon
tench
tiddler
tuna
tunny
turbot
whelk
whitebait
whiting
winkle

Alcohol
(a selection)

absinthe	Calvados	grenadine	porter
advocaat	Campari	Guinness	punch
ale	Chablis	hock	Riesling
amontillado	Chambertin	hollands	Rhenish
Angostura	champagne	hootch	Rioja
anisette	(*see* CHAMPAGNE)	kümmel	rosé
Armagnac	charneco	Kvass	rouge
arrack	chartreuse	lager	rum
Asti	chianti	Liebfraumilch	rye
barley wine	cider	Macon	sack
Bass	Cinzano	Madeira	saki
Beaujolais	claret	malmsey	Sauternes
Beaune	Cognac	malt	schnap(p)s
beer	Cointreau	Manhattan	scotch
Benedictine	creme de menthe	marschino	sherry
(*see* MONKS)	curaçao	Marsala	slivovitz
bitter(s)	daiquiri	Martini	stingo
blanc	Drambuie	mead	stout
Bollinger	Dubonnet	Medoc	Tequil(l)a
Bols	Egg flip	moonshine	Tokay
booze	egg nog	Moselle	Usquebaugh
Bordeaux	geneva	Muscatel	vermouth
bourbon	gin	ouzo	vodka
brandy	grappa	Pernod	whisk(e)y
Burgundy	Graves	port	wine

Five Towns

Arnold Bennett's imaginary five towns are:
Bursley Hanbridge Knype Longshaw Turnhill

Wedding Anniversaries

1st: cotton	10th: tin	40th: ruby
2nd: paper	12th: silk	45th: sapphire
3rd: leather	15th: crystal	50th: gold
4th: fruit/flowers	20th: china	60th: diamond
5th: wood	25th: silver	70th: platinum
6th: sugar	30th: pearl	
7th: wool	35th: coral	

Card Games

baccarat
bezique
blackjack
boston
 (*see* US STATES)
brag
bridge
 (*see* BRIDGE TYPES
 THAMES BRIDGES)
canasta
chemin de fer
cribbage
ecarte
euchre
fantan

gin
(*see* ALCOHOL)
gleek
loo
nap
newmarket
 (*see* CLOTHING)
ombre
patience
 (*see* GILBERT &
 SULLIVAN)
pinocle
piquet
poker

pontoon (*see*
 BRIDGE TYPES)
quadrille
 (*see* DANCES)
rummy
sevens
snap
solitaire
solo (*see*
 MUSICAL
 TERMS)
twenty-one
vingt-et-un
whist

Crosses

avallan
botonée/
bottony
calvary
celtic
crosslet

fleury
formée
fourchée
greek
latin

lorraine
maltese
moline
papal
patriarchal

pomée
potent
quadrate
St Andrew's
tau

Arthur's Knights
(a selection)

Accolon	Gaheris	Marhaus	Parsifal
Alphegus	Galahad	Meliagrance	Pinel le Savage
Bedivere	Gareth	Meliot	Sagramour
Blamore	Gawaine	Mordred	Tor
Bliant	Griflet	Patrise	Tristram
Bors	Kay	Palomides	Turquine
Damas	Lancelot	Pellinore	Urre
Ector	Lionel	Peris	Uwaine
Gahalantine	Mador	Percival	

Cheeses
(a selection from the board)

Boursin	cottage	Gorgonzola	Mycella
Brie	cream	Gouda	Parmesan
Cheddar	Double Gloucester	Gruyère	Roquefort
Camembert	Dunlop	Lancashire	Stilton
Cheshire	Edam	Limberger	Wensleydale

Genesis, the six days

1st: light	4th: sun, moon, stars
2nd: firmament	5th: animals
3rd: earth, sea, plants	6th: man

... and on the seventh day He rested.

Seven Sleepers

Constantine, Denis, John, Malchus, Marcian, Maximium, Serapion.

Red Indian Tribes
(a selection)

Apache	Creek	Mohawk	Sioux
Arapaho	Crow	Mohican	Swanee
Blackfeet	Illinois	Navaho	Ute
Cherokee	Huron	Pawnee	Yaqui
Cheyenne	Iowa	Plains	
Choctaw	Iroquois	Seminole	
Comanche	Kiowa	Shawnee	

Peers

Baron	Marquis	Viscountess	Hidalgo
Baronet	Viscount	Lady	Knight
Count	Baroness	Archduke	Noble
Duke	Countess	Comte	Pursuivant
Earl	Duchess	Dame	Seneschal
Lord	Marchioness	Don	Squire

London Theatres

Adelphi	Hampstead	Prince of Wales
Albery	Haymarket	Queen's
Aldwych	Her Majesty's	Royal Court
Ambassador's	Lyric	Royalty
Apollo	Lyttelton's	Salder's Wells
Barbican	Mayfair	Savoy
Boulevard	Mermaid	Shaftsbury
Cambridge	National	St Martin's
Coliseum	New London	Strand
Comedy	Old Vic	Vaudeville
Cottisloe	Olivier	Victoria
Criterion	Orange Tree	Victoria Palace
Dominion	Palace	Warehouse
Drury Lane	Palladium	Westminster
Duke of York's	Piccadilly	Whitehall
Fortune	Pit	Wyndham's
Garrick	Prince Edward	Young Vic

Decisive Battles

The fifteen battles which, according to Sir Edward Creasy (1812–1878), were instrumental in changing European history.

Marathon	Defeat of Varus	Joan of Arc	Saratoga
Syracuse	Chalons	Armada	Valmy
Arbela	Tours	Blenheim	Waterloo
Metaurus	Hastings	Pultowa	

Cloud Types

alto-cumulus	cirro-cumulus	cumulo-nimbus	stratus
alto-stratus	cirro-stratus	nimbo-stratus	strato-cumulus
cirrus	cumulus		

Parliaments

Althing	Curia	Majlis	Soviet
Bundestag	Dail	Poliburo	Stannery
Commons	Diet	Presidium	States General
Congress	Duma	Riksdag	Tynwald
Cortes	Knesset	Senate	Witan

Dinosaurs
(a selection)

allo-	bronto-	mosa-	diplodocus
ankylo-	hadro-	ornitho-	triceratops
brachio-	megalo-	stego-	tyranno-

Dante's Inferno

Vestibule of the FUTILE
Circles of: lustful, gluttonous, hoarders & spendthrifts,
wrathful, heretics, violent, panders & seducers, flatterers,
simoniacs, sorcerers, barrators, hypocrites, thieves,
counsellors of fraud, sowers of discord, falsifiers, traitors.
The above are, of course, in a *descending* order!

Armour

armet	corselet	habergeon	solaret
avontaile	cuirass	helmet	tuille
baldric(k)	cuisse	jesserant	vambrace
basnet	culet	lorica	vamplate
brassard	gadlings	mantlet	vizor
breastplate	gage	morion	
burgonet	gauntlet	pallette	
chamfrain	gorget	plastron	
corium	hauberk	sallet	

Racecourses

Ascot	Fontwell	Newbury	Stratford
Ayr	Folkestone	Newcastle	Taunton
Bangor	Goodwood	Newmarket	Teesside
Bath	Hamilton	Newton Abbot	Thirsk
Beverley	Haydock	Nottingham	Towcester
Brighton	Hereford	Perth	Uttoxeter
Carlisle	Hexham	Plumpton	Warwick
Catterick	Huntingdon	Pontefract	Wetherby
Cheltenham	Kelso	Redcar	Wincanton
Chepstow	Kempton	Ripon	Windsor
Chester	Lanark	Salisbury	Wolverhampton
Devon & Exeter	Leicester	Sandown	Worcester
Doncaster	Liverpool	Sedgefield	Wye
Edinburgh	Lingfield	Southwell	Yarmouth
Epsom	Ludlow	Stockton	York
Fakenham	Market Rasen		

Gods and Goddesses

GREEK	ROMAN	
Aphrodite	Venus	LOVE
Apollo		SUN
Ares	Mars	WAR
Artemis	Diana	MOON
Athene	Minerva	ARTS & LAW
Chronus	Saturn	AGRICULTURE
Demeter	Ceres	FERTILITY
Dionysius	Bacchus	WINE
Eos	Aurora	DAWN
Eris	Ate	MISCHIEF
Eros	Cupid	LOVE
Hades	Pluto	UNDERWORLD
Hephaestus	Vulcan	FIRE
Hera	Juno	CHIEF GODDESS
Hestia	Vesta	HEARTH & HOME
Hygeia		HEALTH
Hypnos		SLEEP
	Janus	BEGINNINGS
Nemesis		VENGEANCE
Nike	Victoria	VICTORY
	Momus	RIDICULE
	Morpheus	DREAMS
	Plutus	WEALTH
	Pomona	FRUITS
Themis		LAW & JUSTICE
	Tellus	THE PLANET
	Terminus	BOUNDARIES
Tyche	Fortuna	LUCK
Zeus	Jupiter	CHIEF GOD

Oracles

Ammon Apis Delphi Dodona Trophonion

Flowers

Acanthus
Aconite
Acorus
Acuba
Agapanthus
Agave
Alyssum
Amaranthus
Amaryllis
Anemone
Antirrhinum
Aquilegia
Arbutus
Areca
Arnica
Arum
Aspidistra
Aster
Aubretia
Auricula
Azealea
Begonia
Belladonna
Bluebell
Bouganvillaea
Broom
Buddleia
Buttercup
Cactus
Calceolaria
Camellia
Candytuft
Carnation
Celandine
Crysanthemum
Cineraria
Clematis

Dahlia
Daisy
Dandelion
Delphinium
Edelweiss
Erica
Flag
  (*see* BANNERS)
Forsythia
Foxglove
Freesia
Fuchsia
Gardenia
Geranium
Gladiolus
Gloxinia
Goldilocks
Gypsophila
Harebell
Heliotrope
  (*see* JEWELS and
  COLOURS)
Hibiscus
Hollyhock
Honeysuckle
Hyacinth
Hydrangea
Iris
Jasmine
Jonquil
Lavender
Lilac
Lily
Lobelia
Lotus (*see*
  CARMAKERS)
Lupin

Nastertium
Nemesia
Oleander
Orchid
Pansy
Pelargonium
Peony
Periwinkle
Petunia
Phlox
Pimpernel
Pink
Poinsettia
Polyanthus
Poppy
Primrose
Primula
Prunella
Rhododendron
Rose
  (*see* ALCOHOL)
Salvia
Sedge
Sesame
Snapdragon
Snowdrop
Speedwell
Stock
Sunflower
Sweetpea
Sweet William
Syringa
Tansy
Tulip
Valerian
  (*see* NOTABLE
  EMPERORS)

77

Columbine
(*see* LOVERS)
Convolvulus
Cornflower
Cowslip
Crocus
Cyclamen
Daffodil

Madder
Magnolia
Marguerite
Marigold
May(flower)
Mimosa
Myosotis
Narcissus

Verbena
Veronica
Violet
Wallflower
Wistaria
Woodbine
Zinnia

Famous Lovers

Antony & Cleopatra
Abelard & Eloise
Dante & Beatrice
Daphnis & Chloe
Dido & Aeneas

Jason & Medea
Paris & Helen
Pelias & Melisande
Pierrot & Columbine
Pyramus & Thisbe

Romeo & Juliet
Samson & Delilah
Solomon & Sheba
Troilus & Cressida
Venus & Adonis

British Universities

Aberdeen
Aberystwyth
Aston
Bangor
Bath
Birmingham
Bradford
Bristol
Brunel
Cambridge
Cardiff
City

Dundee
Durham
East Anglia
Edinburgh
Essex
Glasgow
Heriot-Watt
Hull
Kent
Lampeter
Lancaster
Leicester

Leeds
Liverpool
London
Loughborough
Manchester
Newcastle
Nottingham
Oxford
Queens
Reading
St Andrew's
Salford

Sheffield
Southampton
Stirling
Strathclyde
Surrey
Sussex
Swansea
Ulster
Warwick
York

Cambridge Colleges

Christ's
Churchill
Clare
Clare Hall
Corpus Christi
Darwin
Downing
Emmanuel
Fitzwilliam
Girton

Gonville & Caius
Jesus
King's
Lady Cavendish
Magdalene
New Hall
Newham
Pembroke
Peterhouse
Queens

Robinson
St Catherine's
St Edmund's House
St John's
Selwyn
Sidney Sussex
Trinity
Trinity Hall
Wolfson

Oxford Colleges

All Souls
Balliol
Brasenose
Christ Church
Corpus Christi
Exeter
Green
Greyfriars
Hertford
Jesus
Keble
Lady Margaret Hall
Linacre
Lincoln

Magdalene
Mansfield
Merton
New College
Nuffield
Oriel
Pembroke
Queen's
St Anne's
St Antony's
St Catherine's
St Cross
St Edmund Hall
St Hughs

St John's
St Peter's
Trinity
University
Wadham
Wolfson
Worcester

Campion Hall
St Benet's Hall
Regent's Park

St Hilda's
Somerville

Measurements
(a selection)

1/1000: milli   1/100: centi   1/10: deci   × 10: deka
× 100: hecto   × 1000: kilo

acre	foot	millenium	rod
amp(ere)	fortnight	minim	scruple
angstrom	furlong	minute	second
are	gallon	month	stadium (*see*
bar	gill	newton	SPORTS AREAS)
bushel	grain	ohm	stere
cable	gram	ounce	stild
cental	henry	parsec	stone
century	hour	pascal	tesla
chain	hundred	peck	ton
chaldron	hundredweight	pennyweight	tonne
cran	inch	perch	volt
day	joule	(*see* FISH)	watt
decade	league	pint	weber
drachm	lightyear	pole	week
dram	litre	pound	yard
dyne	lux	quart	year
farad	metre	quarter	
fermi	mile	quintal	

The Twelve Caesars

Julius	Caligula	Galba	Vespasian
Augustus	Claudius	Otho	Titus
Tiberius	Nero	Vitellius	Domitian

Emperors, notable

Antonine	Hadrian	Marcus Aurelius	Trajan
Constantine	Julian	Serverus	Valerian (*see*
Diocletian	Justinian	Theodosius	FLOWERS)

80

Turkish Bath

The various baths originated by the Romans are:
laconicum (very hot), caldarium (hot), tepidarium (warm),
frigidarium (cool).
Disappointingly for some of us, a vomitorium is *not* where
the Romans went to be sick to allow themselves to continue
drinking. It is, in fact, merely the room where the smoke and
unwanted air were got rid of. In other words, a chimney.

Composers
(a selection)

Bach	Glinka	Mussorgsky	Sibelius
Bartok	Gluck	Palestrina	Smetana
Beethoven	Gounod	Prokoviev	Sousa
Bellini	Grieg	Puccini	Stockhausen
Berlioz	Handel	Purcell	Strauss
Bizet	Haydn	Rachmaninov	Stravinsky
Borodin	Hindemith	Ravel	Tchaikovsky
Brahms	Holst	Rimsky-Korsakov	Torelli
Bruckner	Kodaly	Rossini	Vaughan Williams
Chopin	Lehar	Saint-Saens	Verdi
Debussy	Liszt	Scarlatti	Vivaldi
Delius	Mahler	Schoenberg	Wagner
Dvorak	Mascagni	Schubert	Walton
Elgar	Massenet	Schumann	Weber
Faure	Monteverdi	Shostakovitch	Webern
Franck	Mozart		

Teeth

Types of: bicuspids, canines, incisors, molars.
Parts of: cementum, crown, enamel, gum, neck, nerve, root.

The United States and their Capitals

Alabama: Montgomery
Alaska: Juneau
Arizona: Phoenix
Arkansas: Little Rock
California: Sacramento
Colorado: Denver
Connecticut: Hartford
Delaware: Dover
District of Columbia: Washington
Florida: Tallahassee
Georgia: Atlanta
Hawaii: Honolulu
Idaho: Boise
Illinois: Springfield
Indiana: Indianapolis
Iowa: Des Moines
Kansas: Topeka
Kentucky: Frankfort
Louisianna: Baton Rouge
Maine: Augusta
Maryland: Annapolis
Massachussetts: Boston
Michigan: Lansing
Minnesota: St Paul
Mississippi: Jackson
Missouri: Jefferson City

Montana: Helena
Nebraska: Lincoln
Nevada: Carson City
New Hampshire: Concord
New Jersey: Trenton
New Mexico: Santa Fe
New York: Albany
North Carolina: Raleigh
North Dakota: Bismark
Ohio: Columbus
Oklahoma: Oklahoma City
Oregon: Salem
Pennsylvania: Harrisburg
Rhode Island: Providence
South Carolina: Columbia
South Dakota: Pierre
Tennessee: Nashville
Texas: Austin
Utah: Salt Lake City
Vermont: Montpelier
Virginia: Richmond
Washington: Olympia
West Virginia: Charleston
Wisconsin: Madison
Wyoming: Cheyenne

Presidents of the USA and their parties

Washington (Federalist)
Adams (Federalist)
Jefferson (Rep/Democrat)
Madison (Rep/Democrat)
Monroe (Rep/Democrat)
Adams (Rep/Democrat)
Jackson (Democrat)
Van Buren (Democrat)
Harrison (Whig)
Tyler (Whig)
Polk (Democrat)
Taylor (Whig)
Fillmore (Whig)
Pierce (Democrat)
Buchanan (Democrat)
Lincoln (Republican)
Johnson (Republican)
Grant (Republican)
Hayes (Republican)
Garfield (Republican)

Arthur (Republican)
Cleveland (Democrat)
Harrison (Republican)
Cleveland (Democrat)
McKinley (Republican)
Roosevelt (Republican)
Taft (Republican)
Wilson (Democrat)
Harding (Republican)
Coolidge (Republican)
Hoover (Republican)
Roosevelt (Democrat)
Truman (Democrat)
Eisenhower (Republican)
Kennedy (Democrat)
Johnson (Democrat)
Nixon (Repubican)
Ford (Republican)
Carter (Democrat)
Reagan (Republican)

US Presidents Assasinated

Garfield McKinley Lincoln Kennedy

Labours of Hercules

Apples of the Hesperides
Cattle of Geryon
Cerberus
Cerynian Hind
Cretan Bull
Erymanthian Bull

Girdle of Queen Hippolyte
Hydra
Mares of Diomedes
Nemean Lion
Stables of Augeus
Stymphalian Birds

Sea Areas

Bailey	Fisher	Malin	Thames
Bell rock	Fortes	Main Head	Tiree
Biscay	Forth	Plymouth	Tyne
Channel	German Bight	Portland	Utsire
Cromarty	Goeree	Rockall	Valentia
Dogger	Hebrides	Ronaldsway	Varne
Dover	Humber	Royal Sovereign	Viking
Dowsing	Iceland	Scilly	Wight
Fair Isle	Irish Sea	Shannon	
Fastnet	Jersey	Sole	
Finisterre	Lundy	Sumburgh	

Thames Bridges

Albert	Hungerford	Richmond	Waterloo
Battersea	Kingston	Southwark	Westminster
Blackfriars	Lambeth	Tower	
Chelsea	London	Vauxhall	
Hammersmith	Putney	Wandsworth	

Bridge Types

Arch, bailey, cantilever, opening, pontoon, suspension, suspended span, toll, truss, tubular.

Romano-British Towns

BATH Aquae Salis
CANTERBURY Durovernum
CARLISLE Luguvallum
CHELMSFORD Caesaromagus
CHESTER Deva
CIRENCESTER Corinium
COLCHESTER Camulodunum
DONCASTER Danum
DORCHESTER Durinum
DOVER Dubris
EXETER Isca Dumnoniorum
GLOUCESTER Glevum
LANCASTER Lunecastrum
LEICESTER Ratae
   Coritanorum

LINCOLN Lindum
LONDON Londinium
MANCHESTER Mancunium
NEWCASTLE Pons Aelius
PEVENSEY Anderida
ROCHESTER Durobrivae
ST ALBANS Verulamium
SALISBURY Sorbiodunum
WINCHESTER Venta
   Belgarum
WORCESTER Wigornia
WROXETER Virconium
YARMOUTH Magna
   Gernemutha
YORK Eboracum

Phobias
(a selection)

ACRO-: heights
AGORA-: open spaces
ALEURO-: cats
ALGO-: pain
ARACHNO-: spiders
ASTRA-: storms
AUTO-: speaking
BATHO-: falling
BLENNO-: slime
CANO-: dogs
CHROMETO-: money
CHRONO-: clocks
CLAUSTRO-: confinement
DROMO-: crossing roads

ERYTHRO-: blushing
MYSO-: contamination
NOSO-: disease
NYCTO-: darkness
OPHO-: snakes
PANTO-: everything
PHONO-: public speaking
SCOPO-: being seen
TAPHO-: buried alive
THAASO-: idling
THEO-: God
TRISKAIDEKA-: number
   thirteen
XENO-: foreigners

Henry VIII's Wives

Catherine of Aragon (divorced)   Anne of Cleves (divorced)
Anne Boleyn (executed)   Catherine Howard (executed)
Jane Seymour (died)   Catherine Parr (survived)

Nobel Prizes

Nobel prizes are given for outstanding achievement in:
chemistry, economics, literature, medicine, physics, peace.

Shakespeare's Plays
(in alphabetical order)

All's Well that Ends Well   Measure for Measure
A Midsummer Night's Dream   Merchant of Venice
Antony and Cleopatra   Merry Wives of Windsor
As You Like It   Much Ado about Nothing
Comedy of Errors   Othello
Coriolanus   Pericles
Cymbeline   Richard II
Hamlet   Richard III
Henry IV   Romeo and Juliet
Henry V   Taming of the Shrew
Henry VI   Tempest
Henry VIII   Timon of Athons
Julius Caesar   Titus Andronicus
King John   Troilus and Cressida
King Lear   Twelfth Night
Love's Labours Lost   Two Gentlemen of Verona
Macbeth   Winter's Tale

Thieves With Christ

DISMAS, unrepentant   GESTAS, repentant

The names are Greek for SAD and HAPPY.

Roman Legion

A LEGION varied in numbers, but was nominally 6,000 troops. It was divided into ten COHORTS, or sixty CENTURIES. A different division was into fifty or 100 MANIPLES (*see* SACRED ROBES). Officers: GENERAL, MILITARY TRIBUNE, CENTURION (100 men), DECURION (ten men).

Romeo and Juliet

The quarrelling families were, the CAPULETS (Juliet) and the MONTAGUS (Romeo).

Chaucer's Pilgrims

Canon's Yeoman	Friar	Monk	Squire
Carpenter	Haberdasher	Nun's Priest	Summoner
Chaucer	Host	Pardoner	Tapestrymaker
Clerk	Knight	Parson	Weaver
Cook	Man of law	Ploughman	Wife of Bath
Doctor	Maunciple	Prioress	Yeoman
Dyer	Merchant	Reeve	
Franklin	Miller	Shipman	

Horatius

The three men who held the bridgehead long enough for the citizens to smash down the only entrance into the city were: Gate Captain, HORATIUS, and his lieutenants, HERMINIUS and SPURIUS LARTIUS.

This heroic stand led to the saving of the city from the dethroned king, SEXTUS TARQUINIUS, and his Etruscan ally, LARS PORSENA.

This date, 393BC, is the start of the Roman Republic, later Empire.

Government

Some of the CRACIES that have ruled, or we hope might rule.

Aristo-: BEST
Auto-: ONE
Demo-: THE PEOPLE
Dulo-: SLAVES
Hiero-: PRIESTS
Hagio-: SAINTS
Kakisto-: THE WORST
Ochlo-: THE MOB

Pantiso-: EQUALS
Porno-: COURTESANS
Nomo:- THE LAW
Slavo-: SLAVE OWNERS
Staato-: ARMY
Theo-: GOD
Timo-: PROPERTY OWNERS

Tonic Sol-Fa

Doh rah me fah soh lah te doh

Military Academies UK/US

ARMY	NAVY	AIR FORCE
Sandhurst	Dartmouth	Cranwell
West Point	Annapolis	Boulder

Estates

The three estates are KING, LORDS, COMMONS and the fourth estate, PRESS.

Four Freedoms

Freedom from fear and want.   Freedom of speech and worship.

Three Men in a Boat
by Jerome Klapka Jerome

George   Harris   J (assumed to be the author)

Major Racial Groups

American Indian   Caucasian   Melonesian   Negro
Australian Bushman   Indo-Asian   Mongolian   Polynesian

Three Graces
(the Charities)

AGLAEA: brilliance   EUPHROSYNE: joy   THALIA: bloom

Dead Man's Hand

The poker hand held by James Butler, 'Wild Bill', Hickok, when he was murdered in 1876, aged twenty-nine – two aces and two eights.

OK Corral

The gunfight at TOMBSTONE, Arizona, was between the families of the CLANTONS and the EARPS. Among those fighting for the latter were Marshal WYATT Earp, and the murderous dentist and gambler 'DOC' HOLLIDAY. (The Earps won.)

Major Religions

Buddhism   Hinduism   Judaism   Taoism
Christianity   Islam   Polytheism   Shintoism

Typefaces
(a selection)

Antique	Eras	Korinna	Reporter
Baskerville	Eurostyle	Melior	Renault
Bembo	Fruitiger	Microgramma	(see CARMAKERS)
Bauhaus	Futura	Optima	Rockwell
Bodoni	Garamond	Palatino	Roman
Cascade	Gill	Plantin	Souvenir
Century	Goudy	Playbill	Tiffany
Clarendon	Hanseatic	Quorum	Times
Doric	Helvetica	Raleigh	Univers

Typewriter faces are ELITE and PICA.

Musical Terms
(a selection)

accidental
accompany
adagio
agitato
air
allegro
alto
andante
arabesque
aria
arpeggio
bagatelle
bar (see
MEASURES)
baritone
bass (see
ALCOHOL
and FISH)
beat
bow
brass (see
MONEY slang)

bridge (see
BRIDGES
and CARD
GAMES)
cadenza
canon (see
RELIGIOUS
TITLES)
carol
catch
chord
chorus
coda
compass
composition
concert
concord
conduct(or)
crook
cycle
discord
drum
encore

episode
expression
flat
form
glee
grave
harp
instrumental
interval
jig
key
largo
lied
lyre
major (see
COMPARATIVE
RANKS)
minim
minor
motet
movement
nonet
note

octave
opera
oo(us)
organ
overture
passage
piano
pitch
presto
rest
scale
score
sharp
solo (see
CARD
GAMES)
staff
stop
string(s)
suite
theme
tone

Roman Month Divisions

13/15th: IDES   6/8th: NONES   1st: CALENDS

There were no (K)Calends in Greece, hence 'On the Greek Calends' = NEVER.

Apollo II

NEIL ARMSTRONG: Captain and First Man on the Moon.
COLONEL 'BUZZ' ALDRIN: second.
MICHAEL COLLINS stayed in orbit.

Norns

The NORNS approximate to the FATES of Greek and Roman myth, and are:
URD   VERDANDE   SKULD

Carmakers

Alfa Romeo	Dodge	Maserati	Rolls Royce
Aston Martin	Ferrari	Mazda	Rover
Audi	Fiat	Mercedes	Saab
Austin	Ford	Morgan	Skoda
Bentley	Hillman	Morris	Studebaker
Bertone	Honda	Nissan	Sunbeam
Bitter (see	Humber	Oldmobile	Suzuki
ALCOHOL)	Isuzu	Opel	Talbot (see
Bugatti	Jaguar	Packard	FISH)
Buick	Lada	Peugeot	Toyota
Cadillac	Lagonda	Pierce-Arrow	Vauxhall (see
Chevrolet	Lamborghini	Plymouth	THAMES
Chrysler	Lancia	Pontiac	BRIDGES)
Citroen	Leyland	Porsche	Volkswagon
Cowley	Lincoln	Renault	Volvo
Daimler	Lotus	Robin	

Plato's Dialogues

Apology	Gorgias	Meno	Republic
Charmides	Hippias	Parmenides	Sophistes
Cratylus	Ion	Phaedo	Symposium
Critias	Laches	Phaedrus	Theatetus
Crito	Laws	Philebus	Timaeus
Euthydemus	Lysis	Protagoras	
Euthyphro	Menexenus	Politicus	

Paper Sizes

Atlas, Elephant, Emperor, Crown, Demy, Foolscap, Grand eagle, Imperial, Octavo, Post, Quarto, Royal Sixto, Sixmo.

Paper Types

Bank, bond, brief, cartridge, carbon, copy, duplicating, typing, wall, news, wrapping, greaseproof, silver.

Wear
(see also ARMOUR and SACRED ROBES and MATERIAL)

anorak
apron
bags
bandana
bathrobe
battledress
bearskin
bedsocks
belt
beret
bib
bikini
blazer
bloomers
boa
boater
bodice
bonnet*
bowler
blouse
brassiere
breeches
breeks
britches
brogues
buckskins
burberry
burnous
busby
bustle
camisole
cape
cardigan
chaps
chemise

derby
dickie
djellaba(h)
domino
doublet
drawers
dungarees
espadrilles
farthingale
fatigues
fedora
fez
frock
frog
gaiters
galligaskins
galoshes
garibaldi
gauntlet
girdle
glengarry
glove
gown
greatcoat
guernsey
habit
homberg
hood*
hose*
housecoat
jacket
jeans
jerkin
jersey
jodhpurs

mittens
mobcap
moccasins
muffler*
negligee
newmarket
 (see CARD
  GAMES)
nightcap
nightgown
nightshirt
nylons
oilskins
overalls
overcoat
overshoes
panama
pannier
panithose
pantaloons
pants
parka
pelisse
peplum
petticoat
piccadillo
pignir
pinafore
 (see GILBERT
 & SULLIVAN)
plus-fours
pugree
pullover
pyjamas
raglan

shoe
singlet
skirt
slacks
slip
slippers
smalls
smock
sneakers
socks
sontag
soutane
spats
spencer
sporran
stays
stole
stomacher
suit
surtout
sweater
tabard
tie
tights
tile
tippet
toga
topper
trews
trilby
trousers
trunks
tucker
turban
tutu

chiton	jumper	raincoat	tuxedo
choker	kerchief	regimentals	vest
cloak	kilt	ribbers	vestments
clog	kimono	robe	waders
coat	kirtle	rompers	waistcoat
coif	knickerbockers	ruff	wellingtons
collar	knickers	sabot	wimple
combinations	leggings	sandal	windbreaker
comforter	leotard	sari	windcheater
corset	levis	sash	wooll(e)y
cowl	lingerie	scarf	yashmak
crinoline	loincloth	sheepskin	zephyr
cummerbund	mantilla	shift	(see WINDS)
denims	mantle	shirt	

* also CAR PARTS.

BLOOMER is a crosswordese for a flower; BLAZER for the sun. CARDIGAN was a general in the Crimean war. COMBINATIONS were old trade unions. GLENGARY and GARIBALDI are also biscuits. RAGLAN was another Crimean general, SPATS petty fights; a SWEATER is a hard employer, and a TOPPER is the public hangman. TRILBY was the girl hypnotised by Svengali.

Money, the world's
(*see also*, MONEY, SLANG)

afghani	dinar	koruna	napoleon	rupiah
agora	dirham	kreutzer	ngultrum	schilling
anna	drachma	krona	noble	sesterces
as	dobra	krone	oban	shekel
baht	dollar	kruggerand	obol	sixpence
balboa	dong	kwacha	penny	sol
birr	doubloon	kwanza	peseta	solidus
bolivar	eagle	kyat	peso	sovereign
cash	ecu	lek	pffenig	stater
centavo	ekuele	lempira	pistole	sucre
centime	escudo	leone	pound	syli
colon	farthing	Lepton (*see*	pula	tael
copek	florin	SUB-ATOMIC	punt	taka
cordoba	forint	PARTICLES)	quarter	tala
crown	franc	leu	quetzal	talent
crusado	gerah	lev	qitar	tester
cruzeiro	gourde	lilangeni	quadrans	teston
dalasi	groat	lira	real	thaler
dam	guarani	livre	rand	thruppence
dandiprat	guilder	loti	rial	vatu
daric	guinea	louis	riel	won
decime	haler	mark	ringgit	yen
denarius	heller	mohur	riyal	yuan
denier	kina	moidore	rouble	zloty
dime	kip	naira	rupee	

COLON is an intestine, DONG a character with a luminous
nose in a poem by Edward Lear.

Money, slang
(see also MONEY, THE WORLD'S)

ackers	fin	monkey	specie
blunt	gelt	nicker	spondulicks
bob	geordie	pony	smackers
brass	grand	pelf	sawbuck
buck	greenback	quid	tanner
coppers	joey	sou	tosheroon
deaner	lettuce	spanker	tin
dib(bins)	lolly	stiver	ton
dough	loot	shekels	
folding-stuff	mammon	scratch	

Mouldings

baguette (see	beak	fascia	reeding
DIAMOND	cavetto	fillet	scotia
CUTS)	congle	ogee	torus

Gaul

Gaul was divided into three parts under the Romans.

CISALPINE: Italy north of the Apennines
TRANSALPINE: Modern France
TRANSPADANE: Italy beyond the Po river

Military Ranks
(comparative)

AIRFORCE	ARMY	NAVY
Marshal of the RAF	Field Marshal	Admiral of the Fleet
Air chief marshal	General	Admiral
Air marshal	Lt General	Vice-admiral
Air vice marshal	Major general	Rear admiral
Air commodore	Brigadier	Commodore
Group captain	Colonel	Captain
Wing commander	Lt colonel	Commander
Squadron leader	Major	Lt commander
Flight lieutenant	Captain	Lieutenant
Flying officer	Lieutenant	Sub lieutenant
Pilot officer	2nd Lt	Acting sub lt

Monarchs of England
(in chronological order with duplicate names omitted)

Alfred	Henry	Mary	George
Ethelred	Stephen	Elizabeth	Victoria
Canute	Richard	James	
Harold	John	Charles	
William	Edward	Anne	

Seven Hills of Rome

Aventine, Caelian, Capitoline, Esquiline, Palatine, Quirinal, Viminal.

Prime Ministers
(in chronological order with duplicate names omitted)

The office was instituted by George I, who could barely speak English, and began with:

Walpole	Addington	Aberdeen	Baldwin
Wilmington	Grenville	Palmerston	MacDonald
Pelham	Perceval	Disraeli	Chamberlain
Newcastle	Liverpool	Gladstone	Churchill
Devonshire	Canning	Salisbury	Attlee
Bute	Goderich	Rosebery	Eden
Grenville	Wellington	Balfour	Macmillan
Rockingham	Grey	Campbell-	Douglas-Home
Grafton	Melbourne	Bannerman	Wilson
North	Peel	Asquith	Heath
Shelburn	Russell	Lloyd-George	Callaghan
Portland	Derby	Bonar Law	Thatcher
Pitt			

Verona, two gentlemen of

The two gentlemen of Verona were VALENTINE and PROTEUS.

Triumvirates

The first Triumvirate, 60BC: JULIUS CAESAR,
CRASSUS, POMPEY.
The second, 43BC: OCTAVIAN (Augustus), MARK
ANTONY, LEPIDUS.
  Caesar and Augustus both went on to be supreme rulers.

Brands

The officially recognised terms in branding are:

bar	diamond	reverse	tumbling
circle	flying	rocking	walking
crazy	lazy	swinging	

Furies
(Eumenides)

ALECTO   MEGAERA   TISIPHONE

  The Furies were hideous females sent to exact vengeance
from the wicked. The Greeks gave them the flattering name of
'the well-disposed' in order to try and appease them. They do
the same thing with the Euxine sea, a violent and treacherous
stretch of water. Euxine means 'hospitable'.

EEC Members

Belgium	France	Holland	Luxembourg
Britain	Germany	Italy	Portugal
Denmark	Greece	Ireland	Spain

-Isms

A selection of religious and political 'isms':

adventism	determinism	jingoism	quietism
anabaptism	druidism	judaism	racism
anarchism	dualism	lamaism	rationalism
anglicism	ecumenicalism	liberalism	ritualism
animism	empiricism	lutheranism	shintoism
arianism	epicurianism	maoism	sikhism
baptism	evangelicalism	marxism	socialism
bolshevism	evangelism	methodism	spiritualism
buddhism	existentialism	monetarism	Stalinism
calvinism	fascim	mormonism	stoicism
capitalism	fatalism	mysticism	taoism
catholicism	feminism	nazism	Thatcherism
chartism	feudalism	nihilism	theism
chauvinism	gnosticism	nonconformism	unitarianism
communism	hinduism	positivism	utopianism
conservatism	humanism	presbyterianism	vegetarianism
cynicism	idealism	protestantism	veganism
deism	imperialism	puritanism	zionism
demonism	jansenism	puseyism	zoroastrianism

Cinque Ports

Originally: Dover, Hastings, Hythe, New Romsey, Sandwich
Later: Winchelsea, Rye
Limbs: Lydd, Faversham, Folkestone, Deal, Tenterden, Margate, Ramsgate
Lord Warden: Her Majesty, the Queen Mother

Church Interior

Aisle, alter, apse, bema, chancel, font, narthex, nave, transept, pulpit, vestry.

Fates

CLOTHO spins the thread of life
LACHESIS controls its destiny
ATROPOS cuts it

Materials, for clothes

(*see* also WEAR)

acrilan	damask	leather	serge
alpaca	denim	linen	shantung
angora	dimity	lisle	sheepskin
baize	doeskin	mechlin	shoddy
bombazine	drill	merino	silk
braid	ermine	mink	smocking
broadcloth	flannel	nankeen	suede
buckram	flannelette	nylon	taffeta
burlap	fleece	oilskin	terylene
calico	foxfur	organdie	towelling
cambric	fur	organza	tulle
camelhair	fustian	plaid	tweed
capoc	gaberdine	polyester	twill
cashmere	gingham	rayon	velour
chantilly	gunny	sable	velvet
chinchilla	hessian	sacking	velveteen
corderoy	hide	sateen	voile
courtelle	kid	satin	wool
cotton	lace	satinet	worsted
crêpe	lamé	satinette	
cretonne	lawn	seersucker	

Dances

arabesque
barndance
bebop
beguine
bolero
bossa nova
boston
cakewalk
cancan
carioca
carmagnole
chacha
charconne
charleston
conger
coranto
corroboree
cotillion
csardas

fandango
farandole
flamenco
fling
forlana
foxtrot
galliard
gallop
gavotte
gig
gigue
gopak
habenera
hornpipe
hokey-cokey
jig
jive
jitterbug
lambeth walk

lancers
landler
lavolta
limbo
loure
mambo
mazurka
minuet
morris
one-step
paso doble
paul jones
pirouette
polka
polonaise
quadrille
quickstep
rigadoon
rondo

rumba
saltarello
samba
saraband
strathspey
sword
tango
tap
tarantella
turkey trot
twist
two-step
valse
varsovienne
velita
volta
waltz
ziganka

Ecclesiastical Titles

abbé
abbess
abbot
archbishop
archdeacon
ayatollah
bishop
brother
canon
canon minor
cantor
cardinal
chaplain

clerk
curate
curé
deacon
deaconess
dean
eparch
exarch
fakir
friar
imam
lama
metropolitan

minister
minor canon
moderator
monk
muezzin
mullah
nun
pardoner
parson
patriarch
pontiff
pope
prebendary

presbyter
priest
primate
prior
prioress
provost
rabbi
rector
shaman
sister
summoner
swami
vicar

Grammar

ablative
absolute
accidence
accusative
active
adjective
adjunct
adverb
analysis
antonym
apostrophe
article
assonance
clause
colon
comma
conditional
conjugate
conjunction
dative
declension
decline

definite
diacritics (*see*
   PHONETIC
   SIGNS)
diaeresis
dvandva
ellipsis
epistrophe
feminine
finite
fricative
future
gender
genitive
gerund(ive)
gutteral
hyperbaton
hysteron proteron
imperative
imperfect
interrogative
indefinite

infinite
intransitive
irregular
labial
litotes
masculine
meiosis
metaphor
metre
neologism
neuter
nominative
noun
object
onomatopoeia
oxymoron
paragram
parataxis
parse
particle
participle
passive

past
perfect
person
pluperfect
preposition
present
pronoun
semicolon
sentence
simile
subject
subjunctive
subordinate
supine
synonym
syntax
tense
transitive
verb
vocative
vowel
zeugma

Car Parts

(*see* also CARMAKERS)

accelerator
alternator
ammeter
axle
baffle
battery (*see* CRIMES)
big end
blower
bonnet (*see* WEAR)
boot (*see* WEAR)
brake
camshaft
carburettor
chassis
choke
clutch
column
commutator
compressor
condenser
con-rod
crankshaft

cylinder
demister
differential
dipstick
disc
distributor
drum (*see* MUSICAL INSTRUMENTS)
dynamo
engine
exhaust
fanbelt
filter
flywheel
footbrake
gasket
gearbox
gears
generator
governor
halfshaft
handbrake
headlamps
heater

hood (*see* WEAR)
hydraulics
ignition
indicators
jack
jet (*see* JEWELS)
linkage
magneto
manifold
muffler (*see* WEAR)
overdrive
pinion
pistons
points
radiator
reflector
retread
rev-counter
rheostat
rings
rocker
sidelights

solenoid
speedometer
sprocket
stabiliser
starter
steering wheel
stop lights
sump
supercharger
suppressor
suspension
throttle
timing
tonneau
tracking
transmission
trunnion
tuning
tyres
valves
wheels
wipers

Sherlock Holmes

Address: 221a BAKER STREET, LONDON
Brother: MYCROFT HOLMES
Friend: DOCTOR JOHN WATSON, late of the army in Afghanistan
Enemy: PROFESSOR MORIATY
Associate: INSPECTOR LESTRADE of Scotland Yard
Helpers: Young children employed on various duties i.e., 'THE BAKER STREET IRREGULARS' (Leader WIGGINS)
Landlady: MRS HUDSON

Battlements

barbican	loophole	parapet	terreplein
bastion	machiolations	rampart	turret
corbels	merlons	revelin	vallum
crennals	orillion	talus	

Palmistry

Apollo, mount of	Fate, line of	Love
Jupiter "	Fortune "	
Mars "	Head "	Phalanx
Mercury "	Health "	Reason
Moon "	Marriage "	
Saturn "	Heart "	Will
Venus "		

Knots

blackwall hitch	figure eight	sheepshank	slip
bowline	granny	sheet bend	timber hitch
carrick bend	half hitch	square	true lovers'
catspaw	macramé	stevedore's	turk's head
clove hitch	overhand	surgeon's	
fisherman's bend	reef	seizing	

Numbers

billion	decillion	octodecillion
trillion	undecillion	novemdecillion
quadrillion	duodecillion	vigintillion (20)
quintillion	tredeceillion	centillion (100)
sextillion	quattuordecillion	GOOGOL = 1 + 100
septillion	quindecillion	noughts
octillion	sexdecillion	GOOGOLPLEX =
nonillion	septendecillion	1 + GOOGOL of
		noughts

Ecclesiastical Courts

Court for Ecclasiastical causes reserved   Commisions of
Review   Arches Court of Canterbury   Chancery Court of
York   Court of Faculties

The New Towns

Aycliffe & Peterlee	Glenroths	Peterborough
Basildon	Harlow	Skelmersdale
Bracknell	Hatfield	Stevenage
Central, Lancs	Hemel Hempstead	Telford
Corby	Irvine	Warrington Runcorn
Crawley	Livingston	Washington
Cumbernauld	Milton Keynes	Welwyn Garden City
East Kilbride	Northampton	

Supernatural Beings

apparition	fetch	ka	spectre
banshee	flibbetigibbet	kobold	spirit
bogeyman	genie	leprechaun	spook
brownie	genius	lemure	sprite
changeling	ghost	manes	succubus
clurichaun	ghoul	nightmare	sylph
daemon	goblin	oaf	troll
demon	gremlin	peri	urchin
devil	hob	phantom	wraith
djinn	hobbit	pixie	zombie
doppelganger	hobgoblin	poltergeist	
elf	imp	shade	
fairy	incubus	soul	

Herbs and Spices

allspice
angelica
aniseed
asafoetidea
balm
basil
bay
borage
burnet
caraway
cardamom
cayenne
celery

chervil
chilli
chives
cinnamon
clove
coriander
cumin
dill
fenugreek
fennel
fines herbes
garlic
ginger

horseradish
juniper
lemon grass
lovage
mace
marjoram
mint
mustard
nutmeg
oregano
paprika
parsley
pepper

poppyseed
rosemary
saffron
sage
savory
sesame
tamarind
tarragon
thyme
turmeric
vanilla

Crimes
(a selection)

arson
barratry
battery
bigamy
blackmail
bribery
burglary
embezzlement

embracery
extortion
forgery
GBH
hijacking
incitement
kidnapping
larceny

libel
looting
malversation
manslaughter
murder
perjury
piracy
rape

robbery
sacrilege
shoplifting
smuggling
theft
treason

Poets
(*see also* POETS LAUREATE)

Arnold
Beaumont
Beddoes
Benet
Betjeman
Blake
Bridges
Brontë (*see*
BRONTËS)
Brooks
Brown
Browning
Bryant
Burns
Byron
Campion
Carew
Carroll
Chatterton
Chaucer (*see*
CHAUCER)
Chesterton
Clare
Coleridge
Collins
Cowper
Crasaw
cummings

Dante (*see*
DANTE)
Davidson
Davies
De la Mare
Dekker
Dickinson
Dryden
Eliot
Emerson
Flecker
Fletcher
Goethe
Gordon
Graves
Gray
Gunn
Hardy
Henley
Herbert
Herrick
Homer
Hood
Hopkins
Horace
Housman
Hughes
Hunt

Jonson
Keats
Kipling
Landor
Larkin
Longfellow
Lorka
Lovelace
Lowell
Macaulay (*see*
HORATIUS)
Macbeth
Marvell
Masefield
Meredith
Milton
Moore
Morris
Nashe
Ovid
Plath
Poe
Pope
Pound
Prior
Pushkin
Raleigh
Rossetti

Schiller
Shelley
Sidney
Sitwell
Skelton
Smart
Smith
Southey
Spenser
Swinburne
Tasso
Teasdale
Tennyson
Thompson
Virgil
Wain
Watson
Whitman
Whittier
Wilde
Wolfe
Wordsworth
Wotton
Wyatt
Yeats

Volcanos

Cameroun
Cotopaxi
Etna

Fujiyama
Hecla
Manua Loa

Popocatapetl
Mt St Helens
Stromboli

Tristan de Cunha
Vesuvius

Seas and Oceans

OCEANS: Arctic Atlantic Indian Pacific

SEAS:

Adriatic	Black	Java	Ross
Aegean	Caribbean	Labrador	Sargasso
Andaman	Caspian	Ligurian	South China
Arabian	Coral	Marmara	Timor
Aral	Dead	Mediterranean	Tyrrhenian
Azov	Euxine	North	Yellow
Baltic	Galilee	Norwegian	
Beaufort	Irish	Okhotsk	
Bering	Ionian	Red	

Constellations

Andromeda	Coma Australis	Leo	Puppis
Apus	Coma Berenices	Leo Minor	Pyxis
Aquarius	Corvus	Lepus	Sagitta
Aquila	Crater	Libra	Sagittarius
Ara	Cruz	Lupus	Scorpio
Aries	Cygnus	Lynx	Sculpta
Auriga	Delphinus	Lyra	Serpens
Bootes	Dorado	Monoceros	Sextans
Camelopardalis	Draco	Musca	Taurus
Cancer	Equuleus	Octans	Traiangulum
Canis Vernatici	Eridanus	Opiuchus	Tucana
Capricornus	Fornax	Orion	Ursa Major
Carina	Gemini	Pavo	Ursa Minor
Cassiopeia	Grus	Pegasus	Vela
Centaurus	Hercules	Perseus	Virgo
Cepheus	Hydra	Phoenix	Volans
Cetus	Hydrus	Pictor	
Chameleon	Indus	Pisces	
Columba	Lacerta	Polaris	

Notable Stars

Achenar	Betelgeuse	Fomalhaut	Sirius
Altair	Canopus	Polaris	Spica
Aldeberan	Capella	Pollux	Vega
Antares	Centaurus	Procyon	
Arcturus	Deneb	Rigel	

Planets and Satellites

The planets without satellites are MERCURY and VENUS.
EARTH has one, LUNA.

MARS	JUPITER	SATURN	URANUS	NEPTUNE	PLUTO
Deimos	Amalthea	Atlas	Ariel	Nereid	Charon
Phobos	Ananke	Calypso	Miranda	Triton	
	Adrastea	Dione	Oberon		
	Callisto	Enceladus	Titania		
	Carme	Epimetheus	Umbriel		
	Elara	Hyperion			
	Europa	Iapetus			
	Ganymede	Janus			
	Himalia	Mimas			
	Io	Phoebe			
	Leda	Rhea			
	Lysithea	Tellesto			
	Metis	Tithys			
	Pasiphae	Titan			
	Sinope				
	Thebe				

Sermon on the Mount

Blessed are the poor in spirit, for theirs is the kingdom of Heaven
Blessed are they that mourn, for they shall be comforted
Blessed are the meek, for they shall inherit the earth
Blessed are they who hunger and thirst after righteousness, for they shall be filled
Blessed are the merciful, for they shall receive mercy
Blessed are the pure in heart, for they shall see God
Blessed are the peacemakers, for they shall be called the children of God

Dogs

afghan	chow (chow)	irish setter	schnauzer
airedale	cocker spaniel	irish wolfhound	scotch terrier
alsatian	collie	kelpie	sealyham
basenji	corgi	King Charles	setter
basset	dachshund	labrador	sheepdog
beagle	dalmatian	lurcher	skye terrier
bedlington	dandy dinmont	maltese	spaniel
bloodhound	deerhound	mastiff	spitz
border terrier	dingo	mongrel	staghound
borzoi	doberman(n)	otterhound	staffordshire
boston	elkhound	pariah	St Bernard
boxer	foxhound	pekinese	terrier
bulldog	fox terrier	pointer	toy
cairn	golden retriever	pomeranian	welsh corgi
cheetah	great dane	poodle	whippet
chinchilla	greyhound	pug	wire haired
chihuahua	griffon	retriever	wolfhound
clumber	harrier	rottweiler	yorkshire
clydesdale	husky	saluki	terrier

111

Birds

accentor
aigret
albatross
aquila (*see*
  CONSTELLATIONS)
auk
avocet
baltimore
bantam
bittern
blackbird
bluebird
bluetit
booby
budgerigar
bullfinch
bunting
bustard
canary
chaffinch
chat
chicken
chough
cock(atoo)
condor
cormorant
corncrake
crake
crane
crow
cuckoo
curlew
cygnet
dabchick
dipper
dodo
dotterel
dove
drake

eagle
egret
eiderduck
emu
falcon
fantail
finch
flamingo
gander
gannet
goldfinch
goose
gosling
grebe
grouse
guillemot
guineafowl
gull
hawk
hen
heron
hoopoe
hornbill
ibis
jackdaw
jay
kestrel
kingfisher
kite
kittiwake
kiwi
kookaburra
lapwing
lark
linnet
loon
macaw
magpie
mallard

martin
mavis
merganser
merlin
moa
moorhen
myna(h)
nightingale
nightjar
nuthatch
oriole
osprey
ostrich
ovenbird
owl
oystercatcher
parakeet
parrot
partridge
peacock
peewit
pelican
pen
penguin
peregrine
petrel
pheasant
pigeon
pippit
plover
ptarmigan
puffin
quail
quetzal
raven
razorbill
redpoll
redstart
redwing

roadrunner
robin
rook
rooster
sandpiper
shag
sheldrake
shelduck
shrike
skylark
snipe
sparrow
starling
stonechat
swallow
swan
swift
tercel
tern
throstle
thrush
tit
titmouse
tomtit
toucan
turkey
vulture
wagtail
waxwing
weaver
whippoorwill
widgeon
woodchat
woodcock
woodpecker
wren
yellowhammer

Jewels
(*see also* COLOURS and HERALDRY)

agate	carbuncle	jasper	ruby
amber	coral	jet	sapphire
amethyst	cornelian	marcasite	sardonyx
aquamarine	diamond	onyx	topaz
beryl	emerald	opal	zircon
bezel	garnet	pearl	
bloodstone	jade	rhinestone	

Sports

archery	cycling	lacrosse	ski-ing
badminton	darts	orienteering	snooker
baseball	dominoes	pelota	soccer
billiards	draughts	polo	softball
bowling	fencing	pool	squash
bowls	golf	racing	swimming
boxing	gym	rounders	tennis
chess	handball	rowing	volleyball
climbing	hockey	rugby	wrestling
cricket	hunting	shinty	yachting
croquet	hurling	shooting	
curling	judo	skating	

Brain

cerebellum	fornix	pons
cerebrum	medulla oblongata	spinal cord
corpus callosum	midbrain	thalamus
cortex	pituitary	ventricle

Diamond Cuts

baguette	culet	marquise	table
bezel	facet	navette	
briolette	girdle	pavilion	

Painters

Augustus John Dürer   Matisse   Sutherland
Bosch   El Greco   Michelangelo   Teniers
Botticelli   Fra Angelico   Millais   Tintoretto
Braque   Fragonard   Monet   Titian
Brueghel   Gainsborough   Munnings   Toulouse-Lautrec
Burne Jones   Gauguin   Murillo   Turner
Canaletto   Giotto   Picasso   Utrillo
Caravaggio   Goya   Pisano   Van Dyke
Cézanne   Hals   Raphael   Van Eyck
Constable   Hilliard   Rembrandt   Van Gogh
Corot   Hogarth   Renoir   Velasquez
Correggio   Hobbema   Reubens   Vermeer
Cox   Holbein   Reynolds   Veronese
David   Larkin   Sargent   Watteau
Degas   Leonardo   Sisley   Whistler
Delacroix   Manet   Stubbs

Cathedral Cities

Canterbury   Lichfield   York   *Wales*
Bath and Wells   Lincoln   Blackburn   Bangor
Birmingham   London   Bradford   Llandaff
Bristol   (Westminster) Carlisle   Monmouth
Chelmsford   (Southwark) Chester   St Asaph
Chichester   Norwich   Durham   St David's
Coventry   Oxford   Liverpool   Swansea and
Derby   Peterborough   Manchester   Brecon
Ely   Portsmouth   Newcastle
Exeter   Rochester   Ripon
Gloucester   St Albans   Sheffield
Guildford   Salisbury   Sodor and
Ipswich   Truro   Man
Hereford   Winchester   Southwell
Leicester   Worcester   Wakefield

Poets Laureate

In chronological order from 1668:

Dryden	Cibber	Wordsworth	Day-Lewis
Shadwell	Whitehead	Tennyson	Betjeman
Tate	Warton	Austin	Hughes
Rowe	Pye	Bridges	
Eusden	Southey	Masefield	

Colours
(*see also* FLOWERS, JEWELS and HERALDRY)

amber	coral	magenta	saffron
amethyst	cream	maroon	sage
apricot	crimson	mauve	salmon
aquamarine	ebony	modena	sandy
argent	emerald	navy	sapphire
aubergine	fawn	obsidian	scarlet
auburn	fuchsia	ochre	sienna
azure	gamboge	olive	silver
beige	gentian	opal	solferino
black	ginger	orange	strawberry
blue	gold	peach	tan
brown	green	pearl	tawny
buff	grey	pink	terracotta
burgundy	hazel	platinum	titian
carmine	heliotrope	plum	turquoise
carnation	indigo	primrose	tyrian purple
cerise	jasmine	prussian blue	ultramarine
cerulean	jet	puce	umber
cherry	khaki	purple	vandyke
cinnamon	lavender	red	vermilion
chestnut	lemon	ruby	violet
chocolate	lilac	ruddy	white
cobalt	lime	russet	yellow
copper	lovat	sable	

Dwellings

abbey
apartment
barracks
billet
bivouac
boarding house
boarding school
bungalow
bunkhouse
cabin
caravan
castle
chalet
chapterhouse
château
condominium

convent
croft
dacha
digs
farmhouse
flat
fortress
garth
gatehouse
grange
guesthouse
hacienda
hall
harem
highrise
homestead

hotel
house
houseboat
igloo
lodge
longhouse
maisonette
manor
manse
mansion
monastery
motel
palace
penthouse
prefab
presbytery

priory
ranchouse
rectory
rooms
roundhouse
semi
seraglio
skyscraper
studio
tent
tepee
towerblock
trailer
vicarage
villa
wigwam

Monopoly Board

In playing order:
Old Kent Road, Whitechapel, Kings Cross, Angel Islington,
Euston Road, Pentonville Road, Pall Mall, Electric
Company, Whitehall, Northumberland Avenue,
Marylebone, Bow Street, Marlborough Street, Vine Street,
Strand, Fleet Street, Trafalgar Square, Fenchurch Street,
Leicester Square, Coventry Street, Waterworks, Piccadilly,
Regent Street, Oxford Street, Bond Street, Liverpool Street,
Park Lane, Mayfair.

Heraldry
(*see also* COLOURS and JEWELS)

accessories	chalice	gules	order
achievement	charger	hind	overt
ambulant	chevron	hippogriff	pale
anchor	cockatrice	impaled	passant
angel	coronet	imperial	pennant
arms	courant	inverted	port
armorial	crescent	issuant	quarter
askew	crest	javelin	ram
axe	decoration	king	rousant
azure	dexter	lion	saltire
badge	ensign	list	sinister
banner	escutcheon	lozenge	tierce
bar	garland	lupus	unicorn
baron	gonfanon	mantlins	vert
basilisk	gradient	martel	vorant
baton	gray	merlon	wyvern
bezant	greaves	motto	woolpack
boar	griffin	olive	

Gulliver's Travels

Lilliput (Little people)
Brobdingnag (Giants)
Laputa (Mad scientists)
Balnibarbi (Mad scientists)
Glubbdubdrib (Sorcerors)
Luggnagg (Struldbruggs)
Japan
Country of Houyhnhnms and Yahoos

Robin Hood's Band

Robin of Loxley, Little John (John Little), Alan-a-Dale, Will Scarlet, Much, the miller's son, Friar Tuck, Maid Marion.

Soaps

Brookside
Coronation St
Colbys
Crossroads
Dallas

Dynasty
EastEnders
Emmerdale Farm
Falcon Crest
Knot's Landing

Neighbours
Sons and Daughters
Sullivans
Young Doctors

Radio: Archers

Astronomers Royal

John Flamstead
Edmund Halley
James Bradley
Nathaniel Bliss
Nevil Maskelyne

John Pond
Sir George Airt
Sir William Christie
Sir Frank Dyson

Sir Harold Spencer-Jones
Sir Richard van der Riet
  Wollley
Sir Martin Ryle

Currently: Professor Graham Smith

Rivers

Adur
Afton
Aire
Aisne
Alice
Allen
Alma
Amazon
Annan
Arun
Avon
Axe
Ayr
Brent
Bure
Cam
Camel
Cart
Cherwell
Clyde
Cole
Colne
Colorado
Congo
Crouch
Dart
Danube
Darling
Dee
Delaware

Derwent
Dnieper
Don
Dovey
Earn
Ebro
Eden
Eider
Esk
Euphrates
Fal
Forth
Frome
Fly
Ganges
Hwangho
Hudson
Humber
Indus
Inn
Irrawaddy
Irwell
Isis
Lea
Lee
Liffey
Loire
Lune
Main
Marne

Medway
Mekong
Mersey
Miami
Mississippi
Missouri
Mole
Murray
Naze
Neva
Niagara
Niger
Nile
Oder
Ohio
Orwell
Otter
Ouse
Oxus
Plate
Potomac
Rhine
Rhone
Rio Grande
Roding
Rubicon
Rye
Saône
Seine
Severn

Shannon
Sid
Somme
Spey
Spree
Suck
Swanee
Taff
Tagus
Tamar
Taw
Tawe
Tees
Thames
Tigris
Trent
Tweed
Tyne
Ure
Usk
Vistula
Volga
Wabash
Wear
Wey
Wye
Yangtse
Yellow
Yeo

Fruit

apple
apricot
avocado
banana
bilberry
blackberry
black currant
blenheim
blueberry
cantaloupe
cherry
clementine
costard
crabapple
cranberry
damson

date
dogberry
elderberry
fenberry
fig
gage
gooseberry
grape
greengage
guava
haw
hindberry
hip
honeydew
huckleberry
hurtleberry

laxton
lemon
lichee
lime
loganberry
mandarin
mango
melon
mulberry
nectarine
orange
peach
pear
pearmain
pineapple
pippin

plum
pomegranate
prune
quince
raisin
raspberry
redcurrant
russet
sloe
strawberry
sultana
ugli
watermelon
whortleberry
worcester

Vegetables

artichoke
asparagus
aubergine
bean
beetroot
broccoli
cabbage
caper
carrot
cauliflower
celery
chickpea
chicory

chilli
chives
courgette
cress
cucumber
endive
gherkin
greens
haricot bean
horseradish
kale
kidney bean
leek

lentil
lettuce
maize
mangelwurzel
marrow
mushroom
mustard
onion
parsnip
pea
pepper
plantain
potato

pumpkin
radish
runner bean
savoy
shallot
soya
spinach
sprout
swede
tomato
watercress
yam

Meat
(principal cuts)

BEEF	LAMB	PORK
best end	breast	gammon
blade	chops	ham
brisket	crown	rashers
chuck	cutlet	trotters
crosscut	patties	
entrecôte	rack	
escalope	riblets	
filet (mignon)	shoulder	
flank		
leg		
loin		
neck		
plate		
porterhouse		
rib		
rump		
shank		
shin		
sirloin		
T-bone		

Months

WESTERN	JEWISH	MUSLIM	HINDU
January	Tishri	Muharram	Chait
February	Heshvan	Safar	Baisakh
March	Kislev	Rabi 1	Jeth
April	Tebet	Rabi 2	Asarh
May	Shebat	Jumada 1	Sawan
June	Adar	Jumada 2	Bhadon
July	Nisan	Rajab	Asin
August	Iyar	Shaban	Kartik
September	Sivan	Ramadan	Aghan
October	Tammuz	Shawwal	Pus
November	Ab	Dhulquadar	Magh
December	Elul	Dhulhija	Phagun

English Counties

Avon	Essex	Nottinghamshire
Bedfordshire	Gloucestershire	Oxfordshire
Berkshire	Hampshire	Shropshire
Buckinghamshire	Herford & Worcester	Somerset
Cambridgeshire	Hertfordshire	Staffordshire
Cheshire	Humberside	Suffolk
Cleveland	Kent	Surrey
Cornwall	Lancashire	Sussex, East
Cumbria	Leicestershire	Sussex, West
Derbyshire	Lincolnshire	Warwickshire
Devon	Norfolk	Wight, Isle of
Dorset	Northamptonshire	Wiltshire
Durham	Northumberland	Yorkshire

Norse Gods

Aegir	Freyia	Loki	Thor
Balder	Frigg	Nanna	Tyr
Borr	Hel	Od	Vidar
Bragi	Hermod	Odin	Wotan
Buri	Hlin	Ran	
Eir	Hod	Sif	
Frey	Honir	Sigyn	

London Train Termini

Blackfriars	Fenchurch Street	London Bridge	St Pancras
Cannon Street	Holborn Viaduct	Marylebone	Victoria
Charing Cross	Kings Cross	Moorgate	Waterloo
Euston	Liverpool Street	Paddington	

Cabinet

The Prime Minister
Home Secretary
Lord Chancellor
Foreign Secretary
Chancellor
Lord Privy Seal
Lord President
Paymaster General
Duchy of Lancaster

Secretaries for: AGRICULTURE,
DEFENCE, EDUCATION,
EMPLOYMENT, ENERGY,
ENVIRONMENT, N. IRELAND,
SCOTLAND, SOCIAL SERVICES,
TRADE & INDUSTRY, TRANSPORT
TREASURY, WALES

The four chief law officers are:
Lord Chancellor (*see* CABINET), Attorney General, Lord
Advocate, Solicitor General.

Continents

Africa, Antarctica, Asia, Europe, North America, Oceania,
South America.

Gorgons

Euryale Medusa Stheno

Insects

ant
aphid
bedbug
bee
beetle
blowfly
bluebottle
bug
bumblebee
butterfly
caterpillar
centipede
chafer
cicada
cockchafer

cockroach
colorado beetle
cranefly
cricket
daddy longlegs
dragonfly
earwig
emmet
firefly
flea
fly
gadfly
gnat
grasshopper
greenfly

grub
hornet
horsefly
housefly
katydid
ladybird
locust
louse
maggot
mantis
mayfly
midge
millipede
mite
mosquito

moth
nit
scarab
scorpion
silverfish
spider
stag beetle
stick insect
tarantula
termite
tigermoth
wasp
water boatman
weevil
woodlouse

Sciences

acoustics
agronomy
anatomy
apiculture
archaeology
astronomy
ballistics
biology
botany
chemistry
cosmology
craniology
dynamics
economics
embryology

entomology
eugenics
geology
geometry
geophysics
harmonics
homeopathy
husbandry
hydraulics
immunology
kinetics
mechanics
medicine
metallurgy
myology

neurology
nosology
obstetrics
optics
osteopathy
pathology
pharmacy
philology
phonetics
physics
physiology
psychiatry
psychology
radiology
rheology

seismology
selenology
sinology
sociology
statistics
taxidermy
toxicology
trigonometry
uranology
virology
zoology
zymology

Moon Phases

New moon, first quarter, full moon, last quarter, waxing crescent, gibbous, waning crescent.

Military Groups

army	detail	maniple	taskforce
battalion	division	platoon	trainband
brigade	echelon	rearguard	troop
cohort	fleet	regiment	unit
command	flight	squad	vanguard
company	group	squadron	wing
corps	legion	staff	

Military Ranks
(non-commissioned)

bombadier	petty officer
chief technician	chief petty officer
colour sergeant	pipe major
commissioned warrant officer	regimental sergeant major
corporal	sergeant
lance corporal	lance sergeant
leading seaman	warrant officer
master pilot	

Feast Days

Ash Wednesday	Good Friday	Whit Sunday	Advent
Quadragesima	Easter Day	Trinity Sunday	Christmas
Palm Sunday	Ascension Day	Corpus Christi	

Christian Names With Double Meanings

Girls

Adelaide	Else	Kit	Pen
Anna	Erica	Kitty	Penny
April	Eve	Lily	Robin
Bee	Faith	Magdalene	Rose
Beryl	Fay	Marigold	Rosemary
Carmen	Florence	Mavis	Ruby
Carol	Gay	May	Ruth
Charlotte	Gene	Merry	Sally
Cherry	Grace	Moll	Sue
Clementine	Hazel	Myrtle	Storm
Columbine	Heather	Olive	Tansy
Coral	Honour	Pat	Veronica
Daisy	Hope	Patience	Violet
Dawn	Iris	Pauline	
Dee	Ivy	Pearl	
Dot	Joy	Peg	

Boys

Albert	Dirk	Jay	Pip
August	Don	Job	Prince
Austin	Duke	Kelvin	Ray
Barney	Earl	Ken	Rex
Barry	Eddy	Kent	Rob
Basil	Frank	Kit	Robin
Beau	Franklin	Lewis	Rod
Ben	Gene	Mark	Sam
Bill	George	Martin	Sandy
Bob	Glen	Miles	Serge
Buck	Grant	Morris	Sidney
Bunny	Guy	Nelson	Stafford
Charlie	Harris	Nick	Storm
Chester	Harry	Oscar	Taffy
Christian	Henry	Paddy	Ted
Clement	In I go!	Pat	Tom
Col	Israel	Peregrine	Victor
Den	Jack	Peter	Warren
Derrick	Jasper	Piers	Will

126

Boxing Weights (WBC)

heavyweight
cruiserweight
light heavyweight
super middleweight
middleweight
light middleweight

welterweight
light welterweight
lightweight
junior lightweight
featherweight
light featherweight

bantamweight
super flyweight
flyweight
light flyweight

Australian Territories

Capital Territory
New South Wales
Northern Territory

Queensland
Southern Australia
Tasmania

Victoria
Western Australia

Art Awards

OSCAR: films EMMY: TV GRAMMY: records
TONY: theatre

Bones

alveolus
atlas
axis
mandible
maxilla
calcaneum
carpus
clavicle

coccyx
coracoid
femur
fibula
humerus
ileum
metacarpus
metatarsus

patella
pelvis
phalanx
radius
rib
sacrum
scapula
sternum

talus
tarsus
tibia
trapezium
ulna
vertebra

Trees

abele	cinchona	ilex	pine
acacia	coconut	juniper	plum
acer	conifer	laburnum	poplar
alder	conker	larch	redwood
almond	cypress	laurel	rosewood
aloe	date	lilac	rowan
apple	deal	lime	rubber
ash	deciduous	linden	sago
balsa	dogwood	locust	sandalwood
banyan	dwarf	mahogany	salix
bay	elder	mangrove	satinwood
beech	elm	maple	sequoia
birch	eucalyptus	may	spruce
blackthorn	evergreen	mimosa	sycamore
bonsai	fig	mulberry	silver birch
box	fur	oak	teak
breadfruit	gum	olive	upas
camphor	hawthorn	orange	walnut
cedar	hazel	palm	willow
cherry	hickory	peach	yacca
chestnut	holly	pear	yew

Literary Awards

Booker
Nobel
Pulitzer

ANAGRAM INDICATORS

A

abandoned
abound
abomination
abstract
about
aberrant
abnormal
abortion
absurd
accidental
acrobatic
actively
adapt
adjust
adrift
addled
adulterated
affect

afflict
afloat
afresh
aftermath of
agony
agitate
all sorts of
à la mode
ailing
alchemy
all over the place
all at sea
all wrong
all over
alias
alien
amazing
amiss

anguish
angry
animated
another
annoyed
analysis
anarchy
anyway
apart
appear
artificial
as a result
around
arch
artful
askew
assemble
astonishing

assailed
assaulted
assorted
at liberty
atomised
at 6s and 7s
atrocious
astray
author of
a bit fishy
about turn
all change
all round
awful
awkward
awry

B

bad
badly
badger
bang
barmy
barney
bash
bashed
bat
batter
battery
beat
become
bedevilled

bedlam
bedraggled
befuddle
bemused
belt
bend
bent
berserk
bibulous
biff
bilious
bit off
blighted
blitz

bloomer
bludgeon
blunder
blur
botch
bother
bouffant
break
breakdown
brew
broach
broadcast
broken
bruise

brutalise
buck
buckle
budge
buffet
bump
bungled
burst
burton, gone
   for a
bust
butcher

C

cancel
caper
carnage
carelessly
cascade
casserole
cast
cast off
cavort
change
chaos
chew
chop
chop suey
chowder

chicanery
chuck
churn
circling
circuitry
cloaking
clobber
cloud
clown
club
clumsy
cobbled
cocktail
collapse
coin

commotion
complicated
compose
concealing
conjuring
cockscrew
construction
contrary
contrive
correct
convert
convulsed
corrupt
crack
crackers

crafty
crazy
created
crooked
cross
crude
crumble
cryptic
cudgel
cuff
curdled
curious
curly
curry
cycling

D

daft	derivative of	disaster	distribute
damage	design	disband	divert
dance	despoil	disease	doctor
debauched	destroy	disfigure	dotty
deceit	devastate	disguised	doubtful
deception	develop	dish	dozy
decoded	deviant	disintegrate	dress
deciphered	devilish	dislocate	drub
defective	devious	disperse	drunk
deform	devise	disrepair	dubious
delirious	dice	disrupted	dud
demented	different	dissected	duff
deranged	directed to	dissolved	dynamite
derelict	disarrange	distort	

E

edit	emend	equal to	excite
edited	emanated from	errant	execrably
eerie	emerging from	erratic	exhibits
effect	enclasping	error	explode
elbow	engineer	escapes from	extract of
elfin	entangled	evil	extravagant

F

fabricated	feverish	foment	frenzy
fabulous	fictional	foolish	fret
fake	fiddle	foreign	frolic
false	fit	forge	fuddle
fanciful	fix	found in	fudge
fantastic	flap	fractured	fulminate
far flung	flawed	fragment	funny
fashion	fling	frantic	fuzzy
faulty	flip	fraud	
febrile	fluid	freak	
ferment	foggy	free	

G

gaffe	generates	giddy	ground
gallivant	genuine, not	gives	gruesome
gambol	gerrymander	gleaned from	guided
gauche	ghastly	going to	gyrate
garble	gibberish	grisly	

H

hack	harrow	haywire	hoax
hammer	harm	haze	horrible
hanky-panky	hash	hew	hotch potch
haphazard	hatches	hiding	hurt
harry	havoc	higgledy piggledy	hybrid

I

idiotic	included in	inhabiting	involved
imbecile	incorrect	injured	irregular
impaired	infamous	insane	irritated
imperfect	infirm	invalid	itinerant
inane	ingredients of	invention	

J

jar	jig	jolt	jumble
jazz	jittery	jostled	jumping
jerking	jog	juggle	

K

kick	kinky	knit	knotted
kind	knead	knock	

I

lark	letters of/from	license	lousy
larrup	liberal	licked into shape	lunatic
leaping	licence	loose	

M

mad	manoeuvre	migrant	monkey with
made from	marshal	mince	mould
maim	mash	mis- words, e.g.	moving
malaise	massage	miscast/treat etc.	muck about/up
malformed	maul	mistake	muddle
maltreat	mayhem	mix	murder
mangle	meandering	mobile	mutant
maniac	mend	model	mutilate
manic	mercurial	modify	mutinous
manipulate	messy	molest	mysterious

N

nasty	nauseous	new	nova
naturally	neatly	nobbled	novel
naughty	negligee	nomadic	

O

obscure	open	organised	over
odd	operate on	originally	overturn
off	order	out	

P

peculiar   plan   possibly   producing
perhaps   plastic   pound   pseudo
pervert   polluted   prepare   put out
phoney   posing as   print out   puzzling
place   position   process

Q

quaking   queer   quirky
queasy   questionable   quivering

R

rabid   really   revolution(ary)   roving
rack   reeling   revolver   rowdy
rage   recipe   rickety   rubbish
ragged   releasing   ridiculous   rude
rakish   remedy   right   ruffle
rambling   repair   riot   ruin
ransack   representing   rip   rum
rash   resolve   rock   runny
ravaged   result   rotary   run wild
ravish   revealing   roughly
re- words   review   round

S

sabotage
sack
salvaged from
satanic
saucy
savage
scatter
scheme
scotch
scramble
scrap
scruffy
sculpted
secreted in
send off/out
senseless
set
shake
shakedown
shambles
shatter

shift
shiver
show off/out
should become
showing
shred
shrouding
shuffle
sick
sifted
silly
sixes and sevens
skipping
slap-happy
slaughter
sling
slip
smash
snap
somersault

sorry state
sort
sozzled
spelt out
spill
spilt
spin
splash
splice
splinter
split
spoil
sportive
spread
squall
squash
squiffy
stabilise
stagger
stampede

stands off/out
state
stir
storm
straighten
strange
stray
strewn
stricken
struggling
stupid
style
submerged in
substitute
surgery
surrenders
swaying
swirl
switch
system

T

tailor
tangle
tattered
tatty
tear
tease
tempestuous
terrible
thereby
therefrom

thrash
throw
thus
tidy
tilt
tip
tipsy
topsy turvy
torment
torn

torture
toss
touched
train
transform
translate
transmute
transpose
travesty
trembling

tricky
trouble
tumble
tumbledown
turbulent
twirl
twist
type

U

ugly	upset	unusual
unorthodox	unruly	use as/for

It is impossible to list all UN words. Almost every verb in the language can have the prefix, and many are used as indicators.

V

vagabond	various	vile	volatile
vaguely	vary	violate	
vandalise	vex	violent	
variety	via	viz	

W

wag	weave	wild	wreck
wander	weird	wind	wrench
warp	whip	wobbly	wrested from
was	whirl	woolly	writhing
way	whisk	work	wrong
wayward	wicked	worry	wry

XYZ

yank	yields
yet	zany

ONE- AND TWO-LETTER GROUPS: ALPHABETICAL LIST

A   above absent acre active adult afternoon
     answer alto amateur ampere ante (before)
     area article associate author austria bomb
     key note
AA   Alcoholics Anonymous or abstainers, non-drinkers,
     temperance people
     Automobile Association or car club, motorists, drivers
AB   jack mariner sailor salt tar
AC   account bill charge current juice
AD   advert bill notice this/our time
AG   silver
AI   capital first class main road
AL   Mr Capone Mr Jolson Young Alan/lad
AM   before noon dawn morning
AN   article
AS   Anglo-Saxon arsenic like while
AT   beside close kind of junction/shirt/square
AZ   everything street guide

B   baron black born bowled British key note
     second rate
BA   bachelor degree graduate pass scholar
BB   Miss Bardot Boys' Brigade
BC   old times
BR   trains

C	about carbon century chapter cold conservative (Tory) hundred number
CA	accountant money man person with bill
CD	diplomats
CE	church
CH	church
CO	care of commander (military chief etc) company firm
CR	credit

D	coin copper day dead degree diamond died five hundred late number old copper
DA	American lawyer attorney lawyer
DC	current
DD	clergyman divine
DE	of France of the French
DI	detective Diana huntress policeman princess
DO	act as before ditto party
DR	doctor medic

E	bearing direction east english (h)e oriental point quarter
ED	editor journalist newsman Ted
EG	for example for instance
EL	the Spanish
EP	record
ER	monarch queen (with) hesitation
ET	and in France extraterrestrial (alien)
EX	earlier former old flame previous lover

F	fahrenheit fellow loud
FA	football/soccer men
FE	iron
FF	very loud
FT	little foot

138

G	George the First gram gravity
GA	Florida state
GB	Britain
GG	child's horse
GI	American soldier foreign soldier
GO	game leave quit turn
GP	doctor

H	aspirate hard height Henry hospital hot hour hydrant type of bomb the centre
HA	hectare
HB	pencil
HE	high explosive
HP	never never sauce

I	myself one
IC	in charge ninety nine
ID	499
IE	that is
II	eleven side team
IL	forty-nine
IM	I am short 999
IN	at home batting fashionable not out
IO	moon
IS	exists
IT	Italian object
IV	four
IX	nine

J	bird we hear
JO	Joel Josephine
JP	magistrate
JR	Dallas man soapy chap

K	king Rex ruler
KC	old lawyer
KG	King George
KO	kick off knockout
KT	knight
KY	Kentucky

L	amateur apprentice fifty learner left liberal many novice number port (left of a ship) or left on board pound (i.e. L.s.d.) pupil quid student tyro
LA	Los Angeles note the French(woman)
LE	the French(man)
LL	fifty/fifty
LO	behold
LP	disc record
LT	lieutenant .
LV	fifty-five

M	Frenchman large number monsieur motorway number thousand
MA	degree graduate mother pass scholar
MC	compère Scotsman
MD	doctor medic
ME	myself yours truly
MI	main road motorway
MM	decoration medal
MO	doctor
MP	legislator parliamentarian redcap service copper
MR	mister
MS	manuscript writing
MY	Lord! gosh! heavens!

N	bearing direction northern point pole quarter
NE	Tyne and Wear (north east England)
NO	Japanese drama refusal

| NT | Bible |
| NY | New York |

O	ball circle duck love nil nothing ring round oxygen old zero
OB	old boy alumnus old pupil
OC	officer commanding
OK	alright
OM	decoration honour
ON	above over running
OO	spectacles
OP	operation work
OR	gold
OT	Bible
OS	large (outside)
OZ	Australia wizard home

P	coin copper page parking penny piano president prince quiet soft
PA	Daddy father
PC	copper policeman
PE	exercise
PI	Greek character
PK	peanuts
PM	afternoon leader Thatcher
PO	Italian flower post office
PP	very quiet/soft
PS	afterthought
PT	exercise
PX	US Naafi

Q	queen question
QC	lawman
QE	liner

R	king monarch queen rex right river
RA	artist(s) gunner(s)
RC	church Red Cross
RD	bounce (of a cheque)
RE	about again concerning engineers sappers regarding
RM	marines
RN	Navy
RR	car Rolls Royce
RT	radio telephone right
RY	railway

S	bearing bob coin direction old Bob quarter Sunday second shilling society south sun Sweden
SE	Kent south east
SF	science fiction San Francisco
SH	hush
SI	Spanish yes
SO	thus
SP	odds
SS	Nazis ship vessel
ST	Holy man saint way
SW	Cornwall

T	junction shirt square
TA	army terriers thanks
TO	at towards
TT	abstainer race teetotal
TV	set

U	fashionable type of boat university
UK	Britain
UN	World Council multinational company
UR	old city
US	America United States you and me unserviceable

V	against five number versus victory
VA	museum state Virginia
VC	award decoration
VE	day of victory
VI	six
VJ	day of victory
VP	vice president

W	bearing direction point quarter Welsh west(ern)
WE	you and I us
WG	cricketer Mr Grace
WI	women's group

X	cross kiss number ten unknown vote
XI	eleven side team
XL	forty
XV	fifteen rugby team
XX	twenty top brew

Y	yard year yen
YC	young con/Tory

Z	last letter omega zero
ZZ	asleep

INDEX TO LISTS

ACADEMY
  Awards 127
  Military 88
AGES, geological 64
AGES, Seven of man 63
ALCOHOL 70
ALPHABET, Greek 62
AMERICA
  Assassinations 83
  Presidents 83
  States/Capitals 82
ANNIVERSARIES, wedding 71
APOCRYPHA 66
APOLLO II 91
APOSTLES 64
ARGO 65
ARMOUR 75
ARTHUR, King 72
ARTIFICIAL LANGUAGES 55
ARTISTS 114
ASSASSINATIONS, US 83
ASTRONAUTS 91
ASTRONOMERS, Royal 118
ATMOSPHERE 68
ATOM PARTS 62
AUSTRALIA 127
AWARDS
  Academy 127
  Civil 57
  Literary 128
  Military 88

BATHS, Turkish 81
BATTLEMENTS 105
BATTLES, fifteen decisive 74
BEAUFORT SCALE 57

BENNETT, Arnold 70
BIBLE
  Apocrypha 66
  Genesis 72
  New Testament 66
  Old Testament 66
  (see also CHRIST)
BIRDS 112
BOAT, three men in a 89
BONES 127
BOOKS, Dewey 58
BOTTLES, sizes 65
BOXING, weights 127
BRAIN PARTS 113
BRANDS 99
BRIDGES
  Thames 84
  Types 84
BRITISH UNIVERSITIES 78
BRONTËS 59

CABAL 65
CABINET 123
CAESARS, Twelve 80
CALENDARS
  French Revolution 63
  Hindu 121
  Jewish 121
  Moslem 121
CAMBRIDGE UNIV. 79
CANADA 62
CANONICAL HOURS 63
CARS
  Makers 91
  Parts 104
CARD GAMES 71

CATHEDRAL CITIES 114
CHAMPAGNE BOTTLES 65
CHARITIES/Graces 89
CHAUCER'S PILGRIMS 87
CHEESES 72
CHINESE YEARS 56
CHRIST
  Apostles 64
  Sermon on the Mount 111
  Thieves with 86
CHURCH
  Courts 106
  Interior 100
  Robes 67
  Titles 102
CINQUE PORTS 100
CLOTHES
  Materials 101
CLOUD, types 74
COLOURS 115
COMMON MARKET 99
COMPOSERS 81
CONSTELLATIONS
  Stars 109
COOKING, ways of 57
COUNTIES 122
CREASY, Edward 74
CRICKET, positions 59
CRIMES 107
CROSSES 71
CUTS
  Diamonds 113
  Meat 121

DANCES 102
DANTE'S INFERNO 75
DEADLY SINS 67
DEAD MAN'S HAND 89
DECORATIONS
  Civil 57
  Military 57
DEWEY SYSTEM 58
DIACRITICS 64
DIAMOND CUTS 113
DICKENS' NOVELS 58
DINOSAURS 74
DOGS 111
DRINK 70

DWARFS, the seven 64
DWELLINGS 116

ECCLESIASTICAL
  Robes 67
  Titles 102
EEC MEMBERS 99
ELEMENTS 61
EMPERORS, Roman 80
ENGLISH COUNTIES 122
ESTATES, the four 88

FATES 101
FEAST DAYS 125
FISH 69
FIVE TOWNS 70
FLOWERS 77
  Parts 67
FOUR ESTATES 88
FOUR FREEDOMS 88
FRENCH REVOLUTIONARY
  CALENDAR 63
FRUIT 120
FURIES 99

GANGSTERS 62
GASES, rare 56
GAUL, the three parts 96
GENESIS 72
GEOLOGICAL AGES 64
GHOSTS 106
GILBERT & SULLIVAN 68
GODS
  Greek 76
  Roman 76
  Norse 122
GORGONS 123
GOVERNMENT TYPES 88
  (see also PARLIAMENTS)
GRACES/Charities 89
GRAMMAR 103
GREEK
  Alphabet 62
  Gods 76
GULLIVER 117

HENRY VIII, wives 86
HERALDRY 117

HERBS 107
HERCULES, labours 83
HICKOK, Wild Bill 89
HILLS, the seven 98
HINDU MONTHS 121
HOMES 56
HOOD, Robin 117
HORATIUS 87
HORSEMEN, the four 65
HORSE PARTS 58

INDIANS, red 73
INFERNO, hells 75
INNS, of court 55
INSECTS 124
INSTRUMENTS, musical 68
-ISMS 100

JASON 65
JEROME K. JEROME 89
JEWELLERY 113
JEWISH MONTHS 121
JUDGEMENT OF PARIS 64
JUDGES 56

KING ARTHUR 72
KINGS, of England 97
KNIGHTS, Arthur's 72
KNOTS 105

LABOURS, Hercules 83
LANGUAGE
  Artificial 55
  Grammar 103
LAUREATES, poet 115
LAW
  Judges 56
  Sittings 62
LEGION, Roman 87
LITERARY AWARDS 128
LIVERY COMPANIES 67
LONDON
  Bridges 84
  Stations 122
  Theatres 73
LOVERS, famous 78

MATERIALS, to wear 101

MEASUREMENTS 80
MEAT CUTS 121
MEDALS 57
MILITARY
  Academies 88
  Armour 75
  Battlements 105
  Groups 125
  NCOs 125
  Ranks 97
MONEY, slang 96
Money, world 95
MONKS 55
MONTHS
  French Revolution 63
  Hindu 121
  Jewish 121
  Moslem 121
MONOPOLY BOARD 116
MOON PHASES 125
MOSLEM MONTHS 121
MOULDINGS 96
MUSES 63
MUSIC
  Composers 81
  Instruments 68
  Terms 90
MUSKETEERS, the three 66
MYTHS
  Greek/Roman 76
  Norse 122
  Oracles 76

NAMES, double meaning 126
NEW TESTAMENT 66
NEW TOWNS 106
NOBEL PRIZES 86
NORNS 91
NORSE GODS 122
NUMBERS 105

OCEANS 109
OK CORRAL 89
OLD TESTAMENT 66
OPERAS, Gilbert & Sullivan 68
ORACLES 76
ORDERS
  Civil 73

Military 97
Monastic 55
OXFORD UNIVERSITY 79

PAINTERS 114
PALMISTRY 105
PAPER
  Sizes 92
  Types 92
PARIS, judgement of 64
PARLIAMENTS 74
  (see also GOVERNMENTS)
PARTICLES, atomic 62
PEERS 73
PHOBIAS 85
PHONETIC SIGNS 64
PLANETS 110
PLANTS 67
PLATO'S DIALOGUES 92
PLAYS
  Shakespeare 86
  Shaw 59
POETS 108
POETS LAUREATE 115
POLICE RANKS 65
PRESIDENTS US 83
  Assassinated 83
PRIME MINISTERS 98

QUEENS 97

RACECOURSES 75
RACE GROUPS 89
RANKS
  Comparative 000
  NCOs 125
  Police 65
RELIGIONS 89
RESIDENCES 000
RIVERS
  of Hell 58
  World 119
ROADS, Roman 55
ROBES, sacred 67
ROBIN HOOD 117
ROME
  Caesars, the twelve 80
  Emperors 80

Gaul 96
Gods 76
Hills, the seven 98
Horatius 87
Legion 87
Month 91
Roads 55
Triumvirates 99
UK cities 85
ROMEO & JULIET 87
ROYAL RESIDENCES 56

SACRED ROBES 67
SATELLITES 110
SCIENCES 124
SEA AREAS 84
SEAS 109
SERMON ON THE MOUNT 111
SEVEN
  Against Thebes 65
  Deadly sins 67
  Dwarfs 64
  Hills 98
  Sisters 57
  Sleepers 72
  Virtues 56
  Wonders 63
SHAKESPEARE'S PLAYS 86
SHAW'S PLAYS 59
SHERLOCK HOLMES 104
SHIPS 60
SISTERS, the Seven 57
SITTINGS, law 62
SLEEPERS, the seven 72
SOAPS, TV and radio 118
SPACESHIP, Apollo II 91
SPICES 107
SPORTS 113
STARS
  Constellations 109
  Notable 110
STATIONS, London 122
SUB-ATOMIC PARTICLES 62
SUPERNATURAL BEINGS 106

TEETH
  Parts of 81
  Types 81

147

THAMES BRIDGES 84
THEATRES, London 73
THEBES, seven against 65
THIEVES WITH CHRIST 86
TONIC SOL—FA 88
TREES 128
TRIUMVIRATES 99
TURKISH BATHS 81
TV SOAPS 118
TYPEFACES 90

UNIVERSITIES
  Britain 78
  Cambridge 79
  Oxford 79

USA
  (*see* AMERICA)

VEGETABLES 120
VERONA, two gentlemen of 98
VESSELS 60
VIRTUES, the seven 56
VOLCANOS 109

WEDDING ANNIVERSARIES 71

WINDS
  Beaufort 57
  Names 56
WONDERS, the seven 63

148

HOW TO SOLVE A CROSSWORD

Solving crosswords is a bit like learning to drive; at the beginning it seems to need the brain of an Einstein but, after a little while, we find that it isn't really difficult at all, and that our initial effort has resulted in us having the world at our feet. So it will be with the crossword. After reading this invaluable book the world will never be the same again . . .

About the author

Colin Parsons is eminently qualified to write this magical guide. He has been dubbed 'the Wagner of the word-square'. He has been the resident crossword composer for thirteen years with *The Sunday Telegraph* and *The Scotsman* as well as being the editor of two puzzle magazines, *Quiztime* and *Challenge*. He is also the inventor of a new type of crossword, Upsquares–Downsquares which is now sold all over the world. He has written numerous other books on crosswords as well as being able to use the title British in his trade name – BRITISH CROSSWORD FEATURES – after an appeal to the Minister of Trade and Industry satisfied his criterion of 'pre-eminence in his field'.